MY SPIRITUAL JOURNEY WITH GOD

Navigating the Minefields of Hate,
Racial Prejudice and Discrimination

By:

JAMES BOSTON BUSSELL

Exulon
ELITE

My Spiritual Journey with God
Navigating the Minefields of Hate, Racial Prejudice and Discrimination
by James Boston Bussell

Printed in the United States of America.

ISBN 9781498482356

www.xulonpress.com

To Ben

Best Wishes

as you Continue
Your Journey

James Boston Bussell

2016

Foreword

Navigating the Minefields of Hate, Racial Prejudice,
and Discrimination.

O n first glance at the subtitle of this lively and frank autobiography by James Bussell, one might think there is foreboding ahead, that he will take his readers back down a path of his dreadful struggles and wash his creepy life's cloth, a public uncovering of a bitter man.

To the contrary, this history *cum* memoir might well start off with the declaration: "I had this great life, parents who loved me and my siblings, communities and neighborhoods and extended family that covered me in my formative years, was sharpened as a soldier in Vietnam, in a war that saw the highest percentage of blacks ever to serve in American warfare; and then I married a wife who adored me and gave me children made in Heaven; great jobs and career, a house with a view of the Great Smoky Mountains, and I had a compulsion to write about my life because so much of what lifted me above my beginnings is long gone for black folk." James never fails to credit his faith in God as a basis for the life that has been bestowed on him. Joe Kita, who authored *How to Write Your Memoir* for *Readers Digest*, would be proud.

As his lifelong friend, I have listened to James talk about this book for much of the past twenty-five years, even once when we sat with Pulitzer Prize winner Alex Haley who pushed both of us to "put it down, for the sakes of your children." Alex was especially transfixed by the Appalachian environs that nourished James in his early years – Harlan County, Kentucky – where our fathers entered a coal mine every day in the late 40s and early 50s, until James moved away. He then made his life in urban Appalachia – Knoxville, Tennessee.

Even as much as James and I have in common, this book is hugely eye-opening, very liberating, and therapeutic for me. While he was far from being a trust fund heir, this memoir is not about a hardscrabble youth, not filled with bizarre and unconventional characters. Here you will read about a thoughtful man who has made some sense out of his life and of his inextricable bonds with his loved ones, as well as that of adversaries, of his world.

James shares, in good conscience, his deeply held beliefs and values, how he came to think, feel, and behave. Somebody's going to be wiser and benefit from reading about his experiences. He has woven and translated his involvements together seamlessly, like the pattern in the quilts Appalachian mothers make. He has moved the layers and fragments and pieces around, up from his intuitive recollections, like a great storyteller in the best Appalachian tradition. He pivots, deftly, from stitch to stitch, and nothing is predictable.

This digest of one man's life is such a classic tableau that it could well have started with the words "In the beginning," or "Once upon a time." The expanses of James Bussell's lifetime are not just that of his own, but of an entire generation and it reflects brightly on all of us, with permanency.

William H. Turner, PhD
Editor, *Blacks in Appalachia*

Dedications

To the memories of my parents, Louise and Charles Bussell, retired Col. Frank H. Duggins, Jr. of the U.S. Army, and William "Sonny" Davis. These individuals, each in their own way, helped shape me into the man I am today.

To my grandchildren, Nia Boldridge, Jalyn Boldridge, Damien Aye, and Brooklyn Aye. May the spirit of God guide each of you on your journey through life.

Finally, to my wife Karen and our daughters Tara, Stacey, and Ashley. God blessed me with the greatest family. You continue to add so much joy to my journey.

Table of Contents

Introduction

Let me begin by stating that I could not have written this book twenty or thirty years ago. As I approach my seventieth birthday, I can now look back on my life and see in Jeremiah 29:11 where God fulfilled his promise to me: **"For I know the plans I have for you, declares the Lord, plans to prosper you and not harm you, plans to give you hope and a future." (NIV)**

The most significant part of my journey has been demonstrated in how God helped me navigate through life's minefields of envy, hatred, bigotry, racial prejudice, and discrimination. As an African-American, racism has been very much a part of my history. Through His guidance, I accepted racism as a part of life's reality and understood that I had no control over another man's racial prejudices or bigotry. However, I had the option of not empowering such individuals. I refused to allow them to serve as a distraction, by taking me off course from the direction God had planned for me. I never allowed myself to become bitter, nor did I overact to incidences of racism directed at me. A prime example, on a morning after Halloween when we were the only African-American couple living in our neighborhood, I discovered the word "Nigger" spray painted in large red letters on the edge of our driveway. To the dismay of my neighbors, I refused to clean it up. My logic was that, living on a cul de sac, the people driving through the neighborhood would realize that I did not paint "Nigger" on my own driveway. It was more of a reflection on the neighbors than on me. After a couple of weeks, a neighbor met me at the mailbox one afternoon to ask: "When are we going to clean that word from your driveway?" My answer was that, "We (meaning me) did not put it down there and that we were not planning to clean it up." The final outcome will be revealed later.

I have never been bothered by the rebel flag. What is appalling to me is the amount of emotional energy some African-Americans spend in protest over the perceived racist symbol on a piece of cloth. Getting rid of a rebel flag does nothing to improve their well-being. Case in point, The U. S. Department of Education report for 2012-2013 shows that black males have the lowest four-year graduation rate of 70.7 percent.[1] In a 2014 report, the Center for Disease Control reports that 71 percent of black babies are born out of wedlock.[2] Some of our urban communities are beginning to look like Third World countries with high poverty and unemployment rates. How is taking down a rebel flag going to change these conditions in our African-American communities?

In 1999, I had the opportunity to discuss this issue, when I was invited to be a keynote speaker for a conference at South Carolina State University. SCSU is a state-funded historically African-American college located in Orangeburg, South Carolina, forty miles from the state capitol in Columbia. Before my speech, I read there were 1,500 people at the capitol protesting the flying of the rebel flag over the State House. This proved to be a great opening for my talk. I began by saying: "I am not from Missouri. I am from Tennessee. But, can anyone in this room, explain to me how you can get 1,500 people to go to the State Capitol and protest a flag hanging on a pole and you can't get 15 people to go there and request more funding for your state-sponsored university?" This speech opened up a new dialogue with the students, and at the end of the conference I was invited to meet with a student group who was interested in my views on other matters which impact our race. It seemed to me that for the first time, someone of color had encouraged them to open up their minds. I challenged them to stay away from emotional issues and focus on things they could control. My message was that their success can go a long way in defeating racism.

Throughout my life, God has allowed me to confront this racism in a variety of ways. First, He gave me the wisdom to filter out what was racism and what was another person's envy or jealousy. Understanding that all mistreatment of African-Americans can't be attributed to racism, gives you a better prospective on how to respond to a given situation. Throughout my journey, you will find that many of the issues I have faced were perpetrated by members of my own race. In the final analysis, I chose to take the high road and left them to deal with their insecurities and racist attitudes.

With God's help, I have led an amazing life which has been both productive and successful. I have produced a gospel record album for my church's young adult choir. I have produced and hosted a weekly public affairs television show on a local NBC affiliate, which introduced high school students to options as they pondered the career choices they might want to consider. While the emphasis of the television program was to introduce inner-city students to non-traditional careers, the program exposed them to African-American and women professionals. One of my favorite memories from the program was Tony Holder's appearance as a guest. Holder was an African-American pilot who flew for Memphis, Tennessee based Federal Express. On this particular program, the guidance counselor at one of the inner-city schools had identified an African-American student to appear on the program, due to his expressed interest in aviation. During the taping of the show, this student asked Holder and unscripted question: "How do you like your job?" Holder responded: "Young man, I don't have a job, I just fly airplanes." There were over one hundred episodes I produced and hosted without compensation, but with the satisfaction of giving something back to the community.

These things were accomplished through a sound system of values instilled by Mom and Dad. Although Dad died when I was only eight years old, he left behind a legacy through his example. Mom was there to reinforce the idea that we should always strive to be the best at anything we attempted to do. Her favorite axiom: "If you have a task, be it large or small, do it well are not at all."

This journey you are about to take with me almost ended before it began. As an infant, I developed a bronchial infection and the doctors at our hometown hospital in Lynch, Kentucky, had given up on me. They advised Mom that there was nothing else they could do and told her she should take me home. At some point during the death vigil, a neighbor told Mom there was a doctor, twenty-two miles away in Harlan, who practiced herbal medicine. Mom took me to that doctor and he rubbed a salve on my chest. The next morning my congestion had broken, and I am now able to reveal the rest of my journey. Obviously, divine intervention played a part in the discovery of this doctor.

Throughout this book, you will discover that my connection with God is not what you will traditionally find. It is not a communication of constant prayer and it can be best described by physicist Anthony Patch. In a recent radio and podcast talk show interview on *Caravan to Midnight* hosted by John B. Wells,[3] Patch stated that his relationship with God was "subliminal, subconscious and intuitive." This has also been my experience.

Finally, there is no better way to express the significance of my journey than to turn to a quote from Rob Bell, founding pastor of Mars Hill Bible College in Grandville, Montana. Paraphrasing Bell's quote when he says: "I have been told that I need to have faith in God, which is a good thing. But what I am learning is that God has faith in me." [4]

God has lifted me up from a near death experience and presented me with a life that I could have never achieved in my wildest dreams. As an African-American male from a small Appalachian coal mining town, my success did not come easily. My achievements have come from hard work. God's hand has provided me with the wisdom, patience, self-confidence, and, most importantly, the appreciation for His great works and understanding of His control of the universe.

My life offers proof that God has a plan for each of us. We must all place our faith in Him. Allow me to reveal to you how my faith allows me to continue to appreciate God's blessing.

My Old Kentucky Home

My journey began in the small town of Lynch, Kentucky on October 10, 1946. One thing I need to clarify right off the bat is that Lynch derived its name from the U.S. Coal and Coke Company President Thomas Lynch.

U.S. Coal and Coke Company was a subsidiary of U.S. Steel, which at that time was the world's largest steel company. Lynch was built in 1917 on 19,000 acres the company purchased at the southeastern tip of Harlan County near the Virginia border. The coal company was a model for Appalachia in that it provided health care, education, churches, housing, social services, wages and benefits for its workers and their families. The coal produced in Lynch was exclusively shipped to U.S. Steel plants.[5]

Lynch had segregated schools for blacks. U.S. Coal and Coke Co. sought out the best and brightest teachers from the historically black colleges and universities and offered higher salaries to attract them to Lynch. With the emphasis on education, many of this small town's black students ended up in college with some attaining their PhD's. Being a close-knit community, teachers would make themselves available after school to tutor students. It wasn't unusual to find pupils at the teachers' dining room table going over lessons after dinner.

Being a coal mining town, there wasn't a lot to do. I remember participating on a little league baseball team, as well as the pickup tackle football games we sometimes played in the park adjacent to the school. I recall that the Brown family had the first television set in the neighborhood and had cable installed in order to receive a Knoxville, Tennessee television station and a Kingsport, Tennessee station. The television would not sign-on until 6:00 p.m. with the first broadcast being an episode of *The Lone Ranger*. With the only television in the community, you can image how popular the Brown kids were, particularly at around six o'clock. Somehow, most of the neighborhood kids would follow the Brown children home. Mrs. Brown would come into the living room and run everyone out, including me. However, because the Brown family liked me, I would go to the front door of my house, rush out the back door and run through the back yards of a couple of neighbor's homes, arriving at the Browns' back door in time to hear the beginning of Gioachino Rossini's *William Tell Overture*, which was the opening theme for *The Lone Ranger*.

One of my fondest memories of Lynch was sitting on the pool hall steps with the other kids admiring Willis Thomas's new 1956 Ford Thunderbird. Thomas was a former Lynch High School basketball standout who played on scholarship at Tennessee State University in Nashville, Tennessee. After graduating in 1955, he landed a contract with the World Famous Harlem Globetrotters. The community would later produce another basketball star, Benham native Bernie Bickerstaff, NBA player and coach.

My closest friend from my Lynch days is Dr. William Turner. Bill continues to have an enormously successful career as an author, college professor, and most importantly, a promoter of the legacy of Blacks in Appalachia. Bill's writings became an inspiration to the late author, Alex Haley. This was after Haley had achieved his own success with the *Autobiography of Malcolm X* and the historically honored *Roots* for which he received a Pulitzer Prize. Haley was a connection Bill and I had when the famous author made his home in Knoxville.

Bill and I both have had high expectations for our race and have shared the disappointment of a lack of significant progress. We have stood up to the establishment for our beliefs and both have sacrificed our jobs because we chose to hold the establishment accountable for their actions when it came to issues of race. The one thing that Bill and I have in common were strong father figures who would not back down. That will always be the tide that binds us.

Dad, I Hardly Knew Ye

I have a picture of Dad and me strolling down Second Street in Lynch, Kentucky when I was barely able to walk. It depicts the limited relationship he and I had, and also represents the bond of a father and son. At the time of his death in July 1955 at the age of fifty-nine, Dad was looking forward to his retirement and returning the family to Knoxville.

Born in 1895, Charles William Bussell, was a hard working family man. His first wife, Julia, died leaving him with three children, Charles Jr., Zella, and Henrietta. Dad was working in a coal mine in Lynch, and following Julia's death he moved back to Knoxville to be closer to his extended family. Julia's sister Zella Burdine and her husband Horace, helped Dad with raising the children.

He took a job as a butler and chauffeur for the Powell Smith family. The Smith family owned White Lily Flour Co. and had a mansion in the west section of Knoxville. The family employed a number of butlers, maids, cooks, and gardeners.

He would eventually meet and date Mom, Louise Berry. Upon getting married, a number of events were set in place resulting in them moving to Lynch. First of all, Mom gave birth to my older sister Sandra in 1937. Secondly, the African-Americans who worked for Powell Smith decided to ask him for a nickel an hour raise and for Dad to be their spokesperson. Following Dad's request to Smith and during the subsequent meeting he had with the staff, Smith indicated he would take their request under consideration.

A few days later, Smith gave the staff his response. He said the other butler, John, had come to him and told him they did not need a raise so Smith was, therefore, denying their request.

A few days later, Dad drove Smith to the train depot so he could depart for a business trip. It was then that Dad informed Smith he needed to make other arrangements to be picked up when he returned, because he was moving back to Kentucky. Smith asked him to postpone his decision until he returned. Dad replied that his decision was final and he felt disrespected by the response Smith had given the staff regarding the raise. Dad felt Smith did not review the request based on the merits, but used weak comments by a staff member to avoid the real issue. To Dad, that was unacceptable.

I can't image the amount of courage it would take an African-American man in the 1930s to stand up to a prominent white man. He essentially gave up a domestic position to return to the demanding and dangerous job of working in a coal mine. This is an excellent example of the quote expressed by motivational speaker Lisa Nichols. Paraphrasing Nichols, quoting her grandmother on an episode of the *Steve Harvey Television Show,* "Conviction and comfort don't live on the same block; if you want comfort, stay where you are. If you have conviction, you will experience discomfort."[6]

Years later, a number of his former Smith co-workers expressed to me how much respect and admiration they had for Dad and the stand he took that day.

I did not realize that this aspect of Dad's life would have a profound impact on me years later.

Mom told me that Dad was proud to have another son when I was born. Charles Jr. was still in Knoxville with his Aunt Zella and her son Samuel Burdine. Dad and Mom would eventually have three more children Lillian, Larry, and Kenneth.

My memories of Dad are limited. Because of his work schedule and the occasional weekend odd jobs such as house painting that he took to supplement his income, there was not a lot of time left over for interaction with us kids. Frequently, I would find out where he was painting so I could sit on the ground and watch him work just to have an opportunity to be in his presence.

There was one disappointing conversation while sitting on his lap on a rare weekend when he was home. I told Dad how anxious I was to grow up and work in the mine with him. He responded by saying: "Son, if I have any say in this matter, you will never set foot in a mine."

My disappointment was a result of not fully understanding the significance of what he meant.

Not owning an automobile, he would walk us the two blocks to the bus line sometimes on Sunday to take us on the ten-mile round trip bus ride from Lynch to Cumberland, Kentucky. One of the fondest memories of how I attempted to garner as much time as I could with him, was on his occasional weekend trips to Knoxville. A family friend and fellow coal miner, Larkin Banks, worked in Lynch; however, his wife and children lived in Knoxville. He would commute to Knoxville on weekends, leaving after work on Friday and returning to Lynch on Sunday afternoon. Dad would occasionally ride to Knoxville with him to explore housing options as he approached his retirement. When I would ask to ride to Knoxville with him and Mr. Banks, he would initially say, no. He would tell me that he was going to be busy and would not have a lot of time to spend with me on the trip. But I had a strategy: when Mr. Banks pulled up in front of our house, I would start crying. It was obviously painful for Dad to leave me in this state, so he would ask Mom to throw something in a paper bag for me to wear. Now I am on my way to Knoxville with Dad. He and I would spend Friday night at Dad's former sister-in-law Zella Burdine's home.

By the time I was awake Saturday morning, Dad was up and gone. He would arrange for Mom's twin sister Margaret to have me picked up from Aunt Zella's. This would allow me to hang out with my Knoxville cousins and their friends. Dad continued to stay with Aunt Zella; however, I would spend Saturday night with Aunt Margaret. Dad and Mr. Banks would come pick me up Sunday afternoon and we headed back to Lynch. I got what I wanted. Hanging out with Dad and Mr. Banks on the trip from Lynch to Knoxville and back.

One of these trips proved to be more memorable than the rest. The year was 1952 with the Fourth of July falling on a Friday. This allowed Mr. Banks, Dad, and me to leave Lynch on a Thursday due to the long holiday weekend. Sandra was already in Knoxville spending the summer with Aunt Margaret. Mr. Banks and Dad dropped me off at Aunt Margaret's when we arrived in Knoxville, before dropping Dad off at Aunt Zella's.

On this trip, Dad had agreed to take me to a movie. In the process of fulfilling that promise, he came over to Aunt Margaret's house to get me. Our plans were to ride the bus from Bearden to downtown.

As we were about to cross Lyons View Pike to the bus stop, we heard the sound of a siren approaching us. It was an ambulance driven by an attendant from Wheeler Funeral Home, an African-American owned mortuary located in the east section of Knoxville. The ambulance was headed towards Carl Cowan Park, located in deep west Knoxville. It was the segregated facilitate for African-Americans on the banks of Fort Loudon Lake. The park did not have a swimming pool; therefore, the African-American swimmers would dive directly into the lake.

While waiting for the bus to arrive, an African-American gentleman passed us in his car. Seeing us, he stopped and backed up to ask where we were headed. Dad told him downtown. He told us that he was going to pass through downtown and asked us to hop in and he would give us a ride. We had not driven more than a mile when I wondered aloud where that ambulance was going. Dad said he didn't know. This is when the gentleman we were riding with spoke up and said he had just left the park and there was a young boy who had drowned. He said it was one of the Berry boys who lived in Bearden. Dad told the driver the boy was possibly his nephew and asked him to turnaround and take us back to Bearden. When we arrived, Mom's bother Ernest had just pulled up with my cousin Jimmy in his car and he had to tell Aunt Margaret that her twelve-year-old son Cortland, had drowned. One of the neighborhood kids was trying to teach him how to swim and they were not able to resuscitate Cortland.

Dad had a Knoxville friend Mr. Smith (I do not recall his first name) who had a car, and they went to Lynch to pick up Mom and the rest of the family. At the age of five, this was the first funeral I had attended. After the funeral Dad paid Mr. Smith to take us back to Lynch.

Dad was an avid rabbit hunter, and was noted for his marksmanship, being able to shoot the rabbit with his 20 gauge Remington shotgun and not tear the animal all to pieces. He would bring his bounty home and Sandra, Mom, and I would spend an evening dressing and cleaning rabbits. Those were days of good eating at the Bussell household. Mom would cook the rabbits in the best brown gravy with biscuits, rice and green beans. Dad liked sweets and Mom always made sure there was a chocolate cake, banana pudding, or an apple pie in the kitchen for dessert.

On one of his return trips from Knoxville, Mom noticed that Dad's mouth was somewhat twisted and his speech was slightly slurred. She recognized it as a symptom of a stroke. He went to the doctor and Mom's suspicions were confirmed. He was hospitalized with a minor stroke and had additional complications while in the hospital. The doctors did not have the medications in the 1950s to get the causes of the stroke under control and Dad had a major stroke while still in the hospital.

When I began writing this book, I considered the title: "If a Dog Bites You, Life Can't Be All Bad." This title would have represented the second time that I recall God intervening in a profound way. Dad had his stroke in the summer of 1955 and as an eight year old, I knew Mom was spending a lot of time at the hospital with him. She naturally shielded the younger kids from the seriousness of the situation; however, Sandra was now seventeen so she could visit with Dad.

One afternoon, I was playing tag football in the street with the other guys in the neighborhood. Without my knowledge, Mrs. Johnson's dog, Bullet, decided to lie down in the street. As I was backing up to catch a pass, I tripped over Bullet and out of anger, he grabbed my calf with his teeth. My friends were hysterical and hollered that Bullet had bitten Jimmy Bussell. Hearing all the commotion, Mrs. Johnson came out, placed me in her car and took me to the hospital. Mom was already there sitting with Dad.

While waiting for the doctor to treat me, Mrs. Johnson went upstairs to the ward and got Mom to come downstairs to the treatment room. Following the doctor's examination, he determined the dog did not break the skin so I would be alright; however, he encouraged Mrs. Johnson to keep an eye on her dog to make sure it did not develop any rabies symptoms.

As this point, I asked Mom if this was the hospital where Dad was staying. She answered, yes, and I asked if I could see him. She told me that to go to the ward I would have to be sixteen. Since I was only eight, she could not take me to see him. The doctor then intervened, asking if I was Charles Bussell's son. After she told him, yes, the doctor said to take me. In hindsight, I sensed the doctor knew Dad would not get better, and I needed to have the opportunity to see him.

On the way up, Mom attempted to prepare me for what I was going to see. My father was partially paralyzed and had difficulty speaking. When he saw me, I detected a sparkle in his eyes. He was really glad to see me. Mom encouraged me to lean down close so I could hear his now barely audible voice. I grabbed his hand and he told me he wanted me to be a good boy and I would have to be the man of the house to take care of Mom and my brothers and sisters.

Dad passed away a few days later without ever returning home. God's divine intervention allowed me to have some degree of closure with Dad. Although he is dead, I have always felt his presence in my life. Growing up, during conversations with Mom, I would sometimes make a statement and she would look at me and say: "That sounds like something your dad would say." More importantly is my resemblance to him. I have a picture of him in my office at home and a number of people have asked me how I managed to get a picture that makes me look older than I am. I proudly turn to them and say, "That's my dad."

When I was in my thirties, I went back to Lynch to attend a funeral of a former neighbor. While standing across the street from our old home place taking pictures, I heard a voice call out, "Charlie Bussell"? It was Joe Hall, a former neighbor standing on his front porch. He came over and greeted me and said he thought that he had just seen a ghost. He then realized that Jimmy Bussell had grown up to be the spitting image of his dad. He immediately grabbed my arm and escorted me into his house so Mrs. Hall could see the resemblance.

In the final analysis, God's intervention was very prevalent. The dog grabbed my calf and as angry as he was did not break the skin. More importantly, had Bullet not bitten me, I would have never had the experience of saying goodbye to Dad.

Mom brought Dad home to Knoxville where he was buried. A number of Kentucky neighbors were a part of the five-hour funeral procession from Lynch to Knoxville, which was a reflection of how well Dad was liked and respected.

Dad, I hardly, knew ye. Yet, you continue to have an enormous impact on my life.

Family Values and Ferguson–
Meet My Mom

Following Dad's death, Mom alone had the responsibility to shape the future of her children. The 2014 rioting in Ferguson, Missouri, and the events that lead to the unrest there and in other parts of the country, lead me to reflect on my upbringing and how Mom would have responded. This incident inspired me to write the following Letter to the Editor, which was published in the Sunday, December 7, 2014 edition of the *Knoxville News Sentinel*:

> As an African-American, I watched St. Louis County Prosecuting Attorney Bob McCulloch review the results of the grand jury deliberations of the deadly shooting of Michael Brown by Ferguson Police Officer Darren Wilson. As he presented the results, I reflected on my own upbringing and how my late mom would have reacted. My father died from natural causes when I was eight years old. I had an older sister who was about to turn eighteen at that time, and three younger siblings. We all recognized her struggle in raising us with very limited resources. We expressed our appreciation by becoming the kind, considerate, respectful, helpful, and obedient individuals she raised us to be.
>
> With that said, if I had been killed by Officer Wilson under the circumstances described in the aforementioned

deliberations, she would have been disappointed in the loss of her child. She would have been embarrassed to learn that I strong-armed a merchant and took merchandise without paying. However, she would have been even *more disappointed* had I charged at a police officer and placed myself in a situation requiring him to shoot me.

I honestly believe that Mom would have reached out to Officer Wilson and apologized to him for my behavior and expressed empathy for what he was experiencing in the aftermath of the shooting.

Her faith in God would have gotten her through this ordeal. She would not want the demonstrations, peaceful or otherwise; for they would take away from her ability to mourn in peace. More importantly, it would remind her that her son is dead because he strayed away from God's teachings and the values and principles she raised him to follow. The answer for many of the issues facing the African-American community is getting back to traditional family values.

My mom, Louise Bussell, was a principled lady who was very caring and compassionate. She embraced the challenge of raising four children, who were eight years and under when her husband died. Relying on a small pension from Dad's days in the mine, combined with Social Security Survivor Benefits for herself and her children, she made the decision to focus on developing us rather than finding employment to supplement her income. A great decision for the kids, however, a struggle financially.

In August 1956, a little over a year after my father's death, we left Lynch and moved to our new home in Knoxville. Mom's brother, Ernest Berry, had his contractor build a small three bedroom house on land in rural west Knox County that Mom had purchased from him. My uncle had previously used this contractor to build five other houses on property he owned for rental purposes. Mom now found herself with a mortgage on the new home; however, it was a great improvement over the house we left in Kentucky. We had indoor plumbing, including a bathroom, which meant we no longer had to rely on an outhouse. It was a good move for our family. We lived in the same neighborhood as Mom's three brothers, her twin sister, and my two cousins.

Mom had seven siblings and she was most proud of the fact that she was the only one who achieved a high school diploma. For this reason, she stressed education and did not want us to drop out of school like my cousins, who lived a block away had done. Her goal was to have the first college graduates in the Berry family. My older half siblings, Charles and Zella, had degrees from Tennessee State University and Hampton University, respectively. My older sister Sandra was seventeen when Dad died. Knowing that Mom could not afford to support her through college, she felt that her priority was to get a job and become self-sufficient so she forfeited her Kentucky State University scholarship. Her dream of attending college ended with Dad's untimely death.

Mom's value system would not allow her children to accept money for small chores performed for our neighbors. Once a neighbor gave me ten cents for going to the store for her; when I showed Mom the dime, she made me return it to the neighbor. She also would not allow me to caddy at the local country club because she got word that my cousins and some of the other caddies would gamble following a day on the golf course. She did not want me around that element and, as a result, I missed out on a good summer of earnings.

The one time that I really hurt and disappointed Mom, it turned out that God had a hand in that process, as well. While shopping at a local grocery store, an older friend decided to give me a lesson in how to shoplift. He and I both picked up a candy bar and then proceeded to get the item we came to purchase, when we realized that we were being watched and followed by a store employee. In the event they decided to search us, we decided to place the candy bars on one of the shelves as we passed. At this point, we thought we were home free since we were no longer shoplifting.

Not so fast. As it turned out, as we were paying for the items we came to purchase, our neighbor, Mrs. Annie Rodgers, came into the store. She spoke to us as we were leaving. The store clerks, realizing that Mrs. Rodgers knew us, related their suspicions to her. Needless to say, by the time I got home Mom was fully aware of my escapade.

She was both hurt and disappointed. I did not ever want to see that pain I caused her again.

I am thankful that God placed Mrs. Rodgers at the right place, at the right time. This incident involving her was a part of the community support parents received. There was not any hesitation on Mrs. Rodgers's part regarding notifying Mom. That old cliché: "It takes a village to raise a child," certainly applied to our neighborhood. I was heavily impacted by another neighbor in Mr. William "Sonny" Davis. Mr. Sonny's influence came as a result of me hanging out with his sons Edward and Ron. I was typically within ear shot when he would lecture them and give them their life's lessons. He also served as one of the scoutmasters for our community Boy Scout troop. Although he only had a fourth-grade education, I state for the record, that I would give up my college degree in a heartbeat to have his wisdom.

In terms of being a part of the village, Mom was one of the most popular ladies in the neighborhood in both Lynch and Knoxville. She was the person the teens and young adult women could talk to when they were not comfortable speaking to their own parents. The girls knew what they discussed with her was between them and no one else. The guys loved her because she would show up on the playground and compete in pitching horseshoes, winning most of the time. To say she was competitive would be an understatement.

Most week nights our house was the place where my cousins and some of the neighborhood women would come to play the card game, bid whist. Bid whist is a popular game in the African-American community and similar to bridge. On weekends, these card games would last past midnight.

One of Mom's favorite pastimes was enjoying the music of R & B singer Brook Benton. His first hit, *It's Just a Matter of Time*, released in 1959, was her all-time favorite. Giving her Brook Benton's albums provided one ideal way I could express my appreciation to Mom. A special part of my journey with God came in 1977. Benton had scheduled a Sunday evening concert at a local night club, so I reserved a table for Mom and me to attend. During the intermission between the two shows, I sneaked away from our table and went to Benton's dressing room. After introducing myself, I told him I had brought Mom to see him in concert and asked if there would be an opportunity for the two of them to meet. He said anytime a young man would bring his mom to see him, he would come out and meet her. He asked where we were sitting and said he would come out before the start of the second show. I casually walked back to the table and told Mom Benton was coming over to meet her. Of course, she did not take me seriously. After about fifteen minutes, he appeared in the crowd making his way to our table. I gave him my seat. Mom had her idol sitting across from her with her son enjoying this special moment. The conversation ended with him announcing that he had to prepare for the second show. He stood up, leaned over, and gave Mom a kiss on the cheek. Her excitement did not end there. As the phone rang the next few days, she would answer, "Guess who kissed me?"

Our relationship with Benton was re-established seven years later. By this time, I was a former executive with the Tennessee Valley Authority. The Quality Inn Hotel was across the street from the TVA complex. While at TVA, I frequently ate lunch in their dining room and was a friend of the banquet manager, Shelia Rucker. While there one day, I noticed a poster announcing that Benton would perform a New Year's Eve dinner concert. I immediately purchased a table for ten. I wanted Mom to share this experience with some family and friends, including Mr. Sonny and his wife Mary. I told Rucker I had met Benton years earlier. Even though I doubted Benton would remember me, I offered Rucker my assistance in helping her host him, if needed.

After spending the afternoon the day before the concert doing radio promotions, Benton opted for a quiet evening in his suite instead of being entertained. But Rucker said he wanted to get reacquainted and asked that I come at seven o'clock and she would escort me to his suite.

It was a very informative and enriching evening, hearing him discuss the entertainment industry. We discussed how he went from a songwriter for the likes of Nat "King" Cole before becoming a performer himself. Benton wrote the mega hit, *Looking Back* for Cole. His introduction to recording for himself came as a result of writing, *It's Just a Matter of Time* for another artist. While recording the song, Brook was not pleased with the artist's interpretation. He entered the studio and sang the song as he would have it interpreted. Fortunately for him, the producer recorded Brook's version and, along with the other artist, convinced him that he should release the song. The rest is history. Brook went from there to record a number of Top 10 and

Top 40 hits. I reminded Brook that in 1961 he was the first R & B act to open the Knoxville Civic Coliseum. He headlined a show with about ten other R & B artists to include the very popular singing group, The Platters.

After about a two-and-half hour visit, I stood up and excused myself. Brook asked if Mom was going to be there for the concert the next night. I said, yes, and that I had a table for ten. He responded that he was going to do something special for her.

On the night of the concert, Rucker had placed my group at a table right in front of the stage. In the middle of his first set, Brook came over to our table and took my seat next to Mom. At this point he placed his head on her shoulder and sang to her. I brought my camera and was able to capture this special moment. During the midnight set, where we all brought in the New Year, his manager came over to me and invited our entire table to come to Benton's suite to continue the New Year's celebration. We hung out with Brook and his entourage until 3:00 a.m. What a memorable evening! This was New Year Eve 1985 and we welcomed 1986 with Benton.

Mom and I were sad to learn of Benton's passing, at the age of 56 on April 19, 1988. Benton's real name was Benjamin Peay. He was born in Lugoff, South Carolina where his funeral and burial were held. An interesting bit of irony, I worked for a U.S. Department of Energy contractor and had to make a business trip to their Savannah River facility in Aikens, South Carolina. I happened to speak to one of the security guards there about my connection with their native son. He indicated that a clerical employee at the plant was a personal friend of Benton and his family. To my surprise, he picked up the phone and called her to come to the guard station. He indicated he had a guy who knew her friend Benton. As I met this lady, she had in her hand an extra copy of Benton's funeral program. I got her address and mailed her photos that I had taken of his performance in Knoxville.

Arriving back in Tennessee, I took Mom her personal copy of her idol's funeral program. She immediately placed it under her glass coffee table in the living room for her visitors to see. Again, what are the chances of this happening without divine intervention?

Eight years later, on March 18, 1996, we said goodbye to Mom at the age of 83. By this time, she had seen my younger sister, Lillian, graduate from the University of Tennessee with a bachelor of science degree. She had seen me complete three years of military service including nineteen months in Vietnam; a son who would enroll in the University of Tennessee at the age of 22 and graduate four years later with a bachelor's of science degree in business administration. The other children had achieved success in their own right. Sandra was employed with the city of Knoxville in the tax assessor's office. Larry was employed as a mechanic with NorthFork/Southern Railroad and Ken was an installer for BellSouth Telephone Co.

I was glad that she lived long enough to see and enjoy my three daughters who affectionately called her "Dese". This happened when my wife and I were trying to determine an alternative name for our kids to call their grandmother. I told her I had inadvertently given her a nickname when we lived in Kentucky that stuck with our neighbors there. As a child, I could not say "Louise" so the sound that came out was "Dese". The nickname lost its appeal when we moved to Knoxville, but was renewed by our children.

The nature of her loss was very inspiring and reinforced our faith in God. Years earlier, Mom had a heart attack which damaged the lower chamber. This area of damage affected the heart's ability to pump, occasionally making it difficult for her to breath. As a result, we had to constantly monitor any build-up of fluids. Even with our best efforts, she still had bouts with congestive heart failure. After one episode, which took place at one o'clock in the morning, she was transported to the hospital in what the doctor described as "very grave condition." After stabilizing her, the doctor acknowledged that she was in God's hands. There was a concern at the emergency room that she would not survive the night. God came through and she lived to be spoiled another day; however, this episode had worsened her overall condition. After two days, I asked the doctor when she would be able to go home. Mom's mind was still very sharp and she was a fighter. The doctor informed me that he had asked a social worker to identify a nursing home to send her to upon discharge. He indicated that she would have to be on oxygen full time as a result of this last episode. This discussion was taking place in Mom's hospital room. I looked at Mom and turned to the doctor and said that Mom was going back to her home. He told me I did not understand. I told him he was the one who did not understand. I let him know that Louise Bussell was our responsibility and that if she needed oxygen to have the social worker arrange to deliver the canisters to her home. Mom was so proud of that moment, knowing that she was going to be in familiar surroundings and that her family was going to be there for her.

Taking care of her became a labor of love for our family. We hired a day sitter for her at fifty dollars a day, Monday–Friday. Each of the five siblings contributed fifty dollars a week for her care. The sitter would arrive at 7:30 a.m. and leave at 5:30 p.m. I would relieve the sitter, and older sister Sandra and her husband Peas would relieve me at 9:00 p.m. and spend the night. On Saturdays, Mom's sister Margaret would spend the day and night. Lillian would spend Sunday nights and my brother Kenneth stayed with her during the day on Sunday. By this time, Larry had moved with his family to Memphis, Tennessee. He would make it a point to occasionally come to Knoxville and spend a week living with Mom as a way of directly participating in her care. This really made Mom feel special.

Mom was determined to stay active. She would bring her oxygen extension cord into the living room and we would compete answering questions along with the contestants on the television game show *Jeopardy* hosted by Alex Trebek. We would spend the balance of the evening competing in the board game Scrabble. She loved working the daily crossword puzzles and enjoyed having me challenge words from her puzzles doing our Scrabble games, resulting in me losing my turn. This was an example of how important she valued her education. She felt confident that she could compete with her college graduate son, and did just that.

I knew how to push her buttons. One evening while playing Scrabble, I said I missed her apple pies. The next day she had Sandra pick-up some apples from the store. The first day she peeled the apples. The second day she cooked them. The third day she made the pastry and put all the ingredients together. When I arrived at her house, there were two freshly baked apple pies on the table. She, of course had a huge grin on her face as she saw my reaction to the pies. She wasn't aware that Sandra had called to tell me that Mom had taken my comment as a challenge. After eating a slice of pie, I turned to Mom and said it was the best "three-day" apple pie that I had ever tasted. We both had a good laugh. I loved that woman's competitiveness.

She passed away on Sunday, March 18, 1996. On the previous Friday, during the nurse's routine home visit, she detected that Mom's heart was out of rhythm. Upon reporting this to the doctor, the conclusion was that the end was near. No time frame was offered; however, the doctor indicated it could be any time. Sandra called me at work and relayed the phone conversation she had with the nurse and said she could not leave her job. I said I would immediately leave work and check on Mom. When I arrived, I sat on the edge of her bed. She asked me if I had heard the nurse's report and the doctor's opinion. I said, yes, and added, "But you are ready aren't you?" Her response was, yes. I responded that we were ready for her, also.

Over the weekend, she would fall asleep and wake up to share dreams of seeing her dead siblings. In one of the dreams, she recalled seeing a shadowy figure standing at the top of a set of steps waving her to come. When she arrived at the top, this shadow turned out to be her deceased Mom.

Sandra and Lillian always spent the night in a twin bed next to Mom. Realizing that Mom's condition was deteriorating, Sandra decided to spend both Friday and Saturday night. Early Sunday morning, she heard Mom say something and she asked her if she needed anything. Mom's reply was that she was talking to the lady sitting on Sandra's bed. Mom said this lady asked the question: "Louise, do you know what time it is?" Mom said: "I told her that it was 4:14 a.m." Sandra looked at the clock and sure enough, it was 4:14 a.m.

It was obvious that Mom was alert and she was being introduced to the angel who was going to escort her on to her new journey. Later that evening, Mom watched the eleven o'clock news and turned off the television. My younger sister, Lillian, was spending Sunday night. Around 1:00 a.m., she became aware of the silence from Mom's side of the room. Mom had peacefully passed away in her sleep. Her journey was complete.

We thank God that He allowed us to spoil her and really express our love and appreciation in those final months.

Family home in Lynch, Kentucky

Entrance to Portal 31 Mine in Lynch, Kentucky where Dad worked

Dad and me walking down 2nd Street in Lynch

Father and Son Comparison

My Profile   Dad's profile

Sister Sandra celebrating my 1st birthday

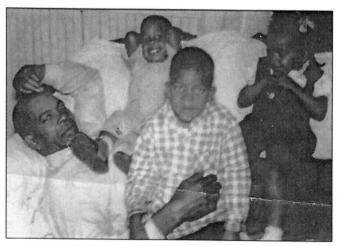

Dad relaxing with Larry (left) me and Lillian

My lifelong Lynch friend Dr. William Turner (left) with my brother
Kenneth during a visit to Lynch

Pulitzer Prize Winning Author Alex Haley with Karen and Me

Louise Bussell (Mom)

(From left to right) Kenneth, Lillian, Larry and Me

R & B Singer and Legend Brook Benton sings to Mom during
New Year's Eve Concert (1985)

Mom's special moment as Brook Benton serenades her

Brook Benton sings to Karen

Celebrating the New Year 1986 with Brook Benton posing in his suite with group from our table. Front row: Evelyn Jack, Karen, and Mom; Second row: Ken Jack, Lizzie Jones (Karen's Mom), William "Sonny" Davis, Benton, Mary Davis and Me

Learning to Love Myself

I t is 1956. While Mom had the challenge of raising her now ten-year-old son, she had plenty of help from God. In 1977, Linda Creed wrote the lyrics to a song entitled, *The Greatest Love of All*. Her lyrics resonated with me thirty-one years following my birth. It turns out that God gave me one of the most precious gifts at an early age–the gift reflected in Creed's lyrics: "Learning to love yourself is the greatest love of all." At the age of ten, as in the lyrics: "I decided not to walk in anyone's shadow. If I fail, if I succeed, at least I'll live as I believe. No matter what they take from me, they can't take away my dignity." This will be reflected throughout my journey with God. My success came through a process where I never compromised my principles and maintained my integrity, and with that, my dignity.

At an early age, I experienced what could be considered bigotry and it came from a very unlikely source–my own African-American neighborhood. Beginning in 1956, as an African-American in the South, I enjoyed the music of Elvis Presley. I refused to be a closet fan and was not ashamed that I would purchase his singles and occasionally his albums. Naturally, I was teased by my friends. This is when I began to hear rumors that Elvis was a racist. He had allegedly made a statement that: "The only thing a Negro could do for him was to shine his shoes and buy his records." I never saw the source of that statement and, therefore, wasn't deterred in my appreciation of Elvis's talents. Sometime later it was published that, while at a Memphis Cadillac dealership, Elvis and his entourage noticed a Negro lady admiring one of the Cadillacs. It was obvious that she was merely window shopping and could not afford the car. Elvis walked over and introduced himself and asked if she liked the car. When she said yes, Elvis purchased the car and gave it to her. How is that for a racist? This was a lesson learned for me: continue the path of being an independent thinker, act on principle, and do not be driven by the opinions of others. While I am sure some of my friends also enjoyed Elvis, but were in denial in the attempt to satisfy their need "to go along to get along." Not me.

This experience helped shape me to become an individual who values standing up for my beliefs, and gave me the courage to accept any barrage of criticism thrown my way. It taught me that others were entitled to their opinions; however, I do not have to be influenced to accept things that I am in disagreement with merely to please others. Yes, as Creed reflected in her song, "this can lead you to a lonely place", and she encourages you to find your strength in love.

Even now as we enter the second decade of the 21st century, many in my race place bigotry labels on people merely because they disagree with their politics. If you are African-American, you become an Uncle Tom should you go against the prevailing thinking in the old neighborhood. You hear it all the time—all Republicans are racists. When U.S. Representative Ron Paul (R-TX), ran for the presidency in 2012, some African-Americans considered him to be a racist. Yet as in the story regarding Elvis and the Negro lady at the Cadillac dealership, Paul delivered the baby of a biracial couple when no other doctors in their Texas community would step up to help the mother and baby. What is most surprising about my assertion, is that when this train of thought is evaluated, there is not much difference between the well-educated African-Americans and the less educated.

As I continue this dialogue, let me be clear, I am an independent with no party affiliation. My goal is to evaluate the total package of a candidate and not focus on one single issues, such as race.

Most of our prominent African-American leaders do not know that it was the Republican Party that pushed the Civil Rights Act of 1964 through the Congress. It was U.S. Senators Everett Dirksen(R-IL) and Thomas Kuchel (R-CA) who helped Democratic Vice President Hubert Humphrey push the act through the U.S. Senate.

Many Americans do not know that the first Voting Rights Act bill was introduced in 1957 by Republican President Dwight Eisenhower. It was titled, "The Civil Rights Bill of 1957." This was in essence a voting rights bill designed to ensure that the Negro could exercise their right to vote. In his 1957 State of the Union Address, President Eisenhower stated the four key provisions of the bill:

- Created a Civil Rights Commission, with a two-year tenure, within the executive branch to investigate civil rights violations.
- Created an assistant attorney general for civil rights and established a Civil Rights Division within the Department of Justice.
- Provided broad language that expanded the Justice Department's authority to enforce civil rights through civil and criminal proceedings.
- Authorized the Justice Department to bring civil lawsuits and obtain preventive injunctions for the protection of voter rights.

The House of Representatives passed the bill on June 18, 1957; the Senate on August 29, 1957 with President Eisenhower signing the bill on September 9, 1957. Then U.S. Senate Majority Leader Lyndon Johnson (D-TX) sent the bill to the U.S. Senate Judicial Committee, chaired by U.S. Senator James Eastland (D-MS), knowing that he would work to water down the bill. South Carolina Democratic Senator Strom Thurmond filibustered for 24 hours and 18 minutes in an attempt to prevent the bill from passing.[7]

President Eisenhower was not finished. In reaction to a violent outbreak of bombings against churches and schools in the South in late 1958, he introduced a second civil rights bill, which was passed on May 6, 1960. One of the significant provisions of this bill was the creation of a permanent Civil Rights Commission. Up until the election of President John F. Kennedy in 1960, African-Americans supported the party of Lincoln, the Republican Party, and for good reason.

Thanks to my ninth grade civics teacher, Mrs. Hudson, I was encouraged to keep up with current events. I continue to focus my attention on things that go beyond what is presented on the major news networks. I want to know, as the late radio broadcaster Paul Harvey would say: "The rest of the story."

Regarding the rest of the story, in late 2015 a childhood friend posted her support for the "Black Lives Matter" movement on her Facebook page. She took exception to the concerns that others raised regarding the amount of "black-on-black" homicides in our urban neighborhoods. She posted that this thinking is a distraction so the nation would not focus on the issues "Black Lives Matters" are raising.

Further she wrote: "We all know that whites kill more people than anybody." I responded telling her she was incorrect. I directed her to the 2012 FBI website where the data on homicides was posted. Of the 12,765 homicides in the United States, 6,454 were black. Of these black homicides, 91 percent (5,873) were recorded as black-on-black.[8] To put this in perspective for her, I said, that over a ten-year period during the Vietnam War, 58,000 soldiers were recorded as killed-in-action. If you look at current FBI data and extrapolate the black homicides in the United States over the last ten years, you will find that there were over 58,000 African-Americans who were killed as a result of black-on-black homicides, more than the total KIA for the war in Southeast Asia over ten years. The message from the supporters of "Black Lives Matter" apparently only apply to those African-Americans killed by white people. The focus needs to be changed.

I have never shied away from tackling the issues facing our African-American communities. In the final analysis, the African-American community has never fully embraced the concept of integration. African-Americans prefer desegregation which is diabolically different than integration. Even Dr. Martin Luther King Jr. spent a lot of his writings making the distinction between desegregation and integration. King said that "desegregation is essentially negative in that it eliminates discrimination against blacks in public accommodations, education, housing and employment—in those aspects of social life they can be corrected by laws. Integration, however, is "the positive acceptance of desegregation and the welcomed participation of Negroes in the total range of human activities."[9]

Integrating myself into the larger society has been a key to my success. Early on as an African-American, I realized that I had to accept the initiative to make whites feel comfortable with me. This is necessary because as a race, African-Americans have done our best to make whites uncomfortable with us. We have confused them in terms of how we want to be defined as a race, whether we want to be called Negro, Black, or African-American. I must admit that there were times when I was confused myself. Whites are intimidated by the need to be "politically correct" and are concerned they will chose the wrong words to express themselves.

Understanding King's push for integration has enormous benefits for African-Americans. Becoming integrated into the larger society,

African-Americans will discover that access to information is critical to one's progression and helps level the playing field. As an example, while attending the University of Tennessee, I chose to join study groups with my white peers. In these study groups, I learned that these white students had networks on campus, with access to certain professors' testing history. In some cases they even had copies of old tests. Did they have an advantage over students that did not have this information? Yes. These are the students I would be competing against in class. At least in these cases, I overcame their advantage. Access to this information and its impact on my future far outweighs any criticism directed at me regarding the methods I chose in pursuit of this knowledge.

In His plans for me, God intervened in my life during my preteen years to teach me to love myself. He prepared me for what was to come. The hurdles I have faced were overcome because of the bond that I have with God and the understanding that He has, as Rob Bell points out, "faith in me."

Tour of Duty in the U.S. Army: Vietnam Experience

One of the best decisions I have made in my life was, at age seventeen, to join the U.S. Army. Many things came into play in making that decision. First of all, the United States had a draft as a part of the selective service process. I would be facing the draft eventually, with most guys getting drafted at ages twenty or twenty-one. Secondly, opportunities were very limited for African-American high school graduates at that time. Most took domestic jobs working as gardeners, golf caddies, hospital orderlies, and similar custodial positions. I had worked those jobs part-time as a teenager. Thirdly, I had seen my older friends finally getting their lives organized and contemplating marriage, when Uncle Sam would send what was referred to as "the greetings letter," their draft for the military. To me, the U.S. Army was a viable option as a possible career. This was 1964 and I was not aware of our presence in Vietnam. Following my enlistment, I did receive knowledge that the United States had approximately 10,000 low-key military advisors in the Republic of Vietnam, and it did not seem there would be any major deployments to the war zone on the horizon. The Gulf of Tonkin Incident, which was the justification for escalating America's involvement in the Vietnam conflict, took place in August 1964 at the tail end of my basic training.

I had one hurdle to overcome to make my enlistment happen. As a minor, Mom would have to sign the authorization for me to enlist. Mom wanted me to go to college and indicated she would not sign the papers. At that time, going to college was out of the question because she could not afford to send me, and I had not prepared myself academically for this path. While I maintained a B-plus average in high school, I avoided all of the college prep courses, especially math and science.

In this regard, I had a humorous conversation with Mrs. Stokes, my high school guidance counselor. She summoned me to her office about midway through my senior year to inform me that I had not taken the ACT. I asked her: "What was the ACT?" She told me it was the American College Test which was given to high school students in order to qualify them for college entrance. I said I had no plans to go to college. She did her best to persuade me to take the test anyway, in case I changed my mind. Realizing she was doing her job and had the best interest of the students at heart, I agreed to take the ACT. This is when she informed me that the test would be given the following Saturday and I should bring ten dollars, which was when I learned how much the test cost. I respectfully declined, telling her I didn't like taking the free exams and I was unwilling to pay ten dollars to take any test. At the beginning of my final high school semester, I had enough credits to graduate, with the exception of English and another mandatory course. I signed up for a typing class to complete a half-day schedule and the principal allowed me to leave school after my morning classes were complete.

I used this time to meet various military recruiters to determine in which branch of the service I wanted to enlist. I decided on the U.S. Army. I was gun-ho and wanted to join the airborne and move on to the Special Forces, commonly known as the Green Berets. The Army recruiter coordinated the military test battery required for enlistment, which determined the most suitable military occupation.

By the time of my graduation in June everything was complete and I was ready to go. Two of my classmates had heard of my decision to join the Army and became interested, as well. Jimmy Brice and Walter Matthews asked me to introduce them to my recruiter and we all ended up enlisting under the buddy plan. This meant the Army would guarantee the three of us would go through basic training together. Brice and Matthews were already eighteen and did not have the parental consent issue that I had.

We were scheduled to graduate on Friday, June 5, 1964. The recruiter informed us he had a basic training class scheduled to begin the week following our graduation. Facing a deadline, Mom had discovered that out of the five classmates from our neighborhood, I was the only one not going to college. She was very disappointed. Mom came to my bedroom where the enlistment papers where on my night stand. She told me what she had learned about the others and said she also wanted me to go to college. She reiterated that she was not going to sign those papers.

This is when God stepped up. I turned to Mom and said: "This decision may determine what happens to me the rest of my life. Years from now when I look back on this decision, whether I succeed or fail, at least I can say it was my choice. As a parent, you owe me the right to make this decision." I do not have a clue about the origin of those words other than divine intervention. It was not something I had prepared in advance. At this point, she grabbed the enlistment papers and the pen next to them, and signed the consent form. She then turned and walked out of the room without saying another word. While I acknowledge she was disappointed, this was the best option for my family and me. The one thing I later realized was that she had already prepared me for the challenges that lie ahead.

I was sworn into the United States Army on Monday, June 8, 1964, three days after I graduated. Brice, Matthews and I completed basic training together at Fort Gordon, Georgia. Matthews and I transferred to Fort Jackson, South Carolina, for our advanced individual training, known in Army shorthand as AIT. Brice was infantry and went to Fort Benning, Georgia.

Matthews and I had been classified as clerks. This is where we had scored highest on our battery of tests. When Matthews and I arrived at Fort Jackson, the Alabama National Guard had been assigned to our training unit. They arrived before the regular army transfers and had been placed in all of the leadership cadre slots. These slots consisted of one platoon leader and four squad leader positions. Keep in mind that this was 1964.

As it turned out, when our unit was asked to provide a detail of men for clean-up around the post, it was always the African-Americans and the one Jewish guy given the assignment. During one of our classes, a regular sergeant came in and asked for a detail to begin painting the exterior of the building where our class was being held. Nick, the

Alabama National Guard platoon leader, selected four other African-Americans, the Jewish guy, and me.

With paint brushes in our hands and buckets of paint, we began the task. This is when I suggested the old concept of "let's not get mad, let's get even". As we were approaching the lunch hour, we knew that all of the units would hurry to be the first in line at the mess hall. Prior to entering the classrooms, we would place our hard plastic helmet liners in order, based on the way we were aligned in formation. We waited about two minutes before the class was scheduled to be dismissed and painted the insides of the helmet liners of platoon leader Nick and his four squad leaders.

Arriving at the mess hall, I asked my squad leader, Private Neely, when was the last time you had a haircut? In response, he raised his helmet liner and ran his hand through his hair only to come up with a hand full of paint. Nick was standing in front of the platoon when Neely informed him that someone had put paint in his helmet liner. Nick became upset and slammed his helmet liner on the ground. At this time Private Neely said: "Nick, they got you, too." The entire platoon burst out in laughter.

Needless to say, a regular sergeant was called and the detail was marched to the orderly room to face the First Sergeant, who we had previously been made aware of the racial problems we were experiencing with the Alabama National Guardsmen. Now he had a detail of five African-Americans and a Jewish soldier. Recognizing the problem, he excused Nick and the regular sergeant. He said there would be no punishment. However, he did need a detail to paint the mess hall interior after it closed for the evening. He offered the reward of a three-day pass. As trainees, we received our weekend passes at noon on Saturdays. This would mean our paint detail would have all day Friday, Saturday, and Sunday off.

That evening we reported to the mess hall around 8:00 p.m. to begin our detail. When we started, a number of guys from the barracks showed up to support us, as they were very appreciative of our antics earlier in the day and wanted to help. The First Sergeant estimated it would take two nights to finish the job. With the help from the other guys, we were done with the entire mess hall around 2:00 a.m. Our help left around midnight to get their rest.

Clean-up took us about an hour. Instead of returning to the bar-racks for the rest of the night, I felt we deserved to be excused from classes for at least the morning sessions. This is when I proposed that we ask the charge-of-quarters to wake us up at 4:30 a.m. The mess sergeant normally arrived around 5:00 a.m. We took our naps on the mess hall tables.

When the mess sergeant arrived, he found us putting the finishing touches on the clean-up and was able to admire his freshly painted mess hall. We got the morning off and the three-day pass. Getting the pass early Friday morning, I headed for the airport and caught a Delta Airlines flight to Knoxville. In 1964, military standby for one-way flights between Knoxville and Columbia, South Carolina, was $6.25. I caught a 6:00 p.m. flight back to base on Sunday, arriving at the unit around 10:00 p.m. All of this from a paint detail prank.

With basic training and AIT behind me, it was time to experience the life of a real soldier. My first assignment following AIT was to Loring Air Force Base, a Strategic Air Command (SAC) installation located at Caribou, Maine. It housed the SAC B-52 bombers. Although I was Army, we were a detachment of soldiers assigned out of Fort Devens, Massachusetts. Our detachment was there to operate and maintain two Army Nike Hercules Missile Sites which served as air defense for the base.

The detachment commander was a Caucasian 1st Lieutenant who had allegedly made a statement that, he would not promote a Nigger as long as he was commander. This statement was obviously directed at me, since I was the only African-American assigned to his unit.

I reported to Sergeant First Class (SFC) Lantis, a Caucasian who was a native of Texas. My job was critical to the maintenance shop where I was assigned. Because of the nature of handling nuclear com-ponents, strong accountability was essential to our operation. Once equipment came into the shop, I was required to catalog it and main-tain an accurate, up-to-date record of the status including, but not limited to, whether it was being repaired, awaiting parts, or ready for the site to pick it up. I maintained a color-coded board, where at any time someone could view it and determine the component's status. Because of the criticality of what we were doing, there would be both announced and unannounced inspections from Fort Devens Headquarters. I would always get 100 percent ratings for my section.

Despite my efforts, it was not unusual for the lieutenant to stick his head in the door of our office to express his displeasure with my performance. He would literally chew me out in front of my fellow soldiers and the civilian workers assigned to our unit. Again, I had the ability to ignore him and not take his actions personally. I merely saw his efforts as a character flaw.

While I was still a private first class (E-3), Lantis had put me in for early promotion based on my performance. The detachment commander rejected that request and its written justification, without forwarding the request to Fort Devens for approval.

After a period of time, Lantis, who lived in the barracks, came to my room to inform me of his efforts. He wanted me to know about the rejection of his request by the lieutenant. He also wanted me to know how much he appreciated the job I was doing. This is when I told him he treated me fairly and I enjoyed working under his leadership. Further, I said I was aware of the lieutenant's attitude towards African-American soldiers; however, Mom had instilled in me that: "If you have a task, be it large or small, do it well or not at all." Then I said I worked for him and I was not going to let the lieutenant get me off my game and the values Mom had instilled in my siblings and me.

A few weeks later, while at a movie theater in nearby downtown Limestone, Maine, I was paged to the phone. It was the CQ calling to tell me I had an emergency at home and I needed to call my sister, Sandra. I called her collect from the theater, and she told me that Mom was scheduled for back surgery to remove a slipped disc the following Wednesday. In 1965, this was considered a very serious and dangerous procedure. Sandra wanted to let me know in case I wanted to come home. This was Friday night and I told her that our unit was having an announced inspection from Monday through Wednesday the next week and that I would try to make it after the surgery.

Following the movie, our group returned to the barracks. A few minutes after returning to my room, Lantis was knocking on my door. The CQ had informed him of my emergency. I shared with him the discussion with my sister that we had the inspection the first of the week and the earliest I could get home would be Thursday after the surgery.

Lantis then said he had already contacted our First Sergeant and that he would be in Saturday morning to cut orders for me to take emergency leave. Then the two of them were going to take me to the airport in Presque Isle, Maine to catch a flight to get me on the journey to Knoxville. He then handed me one hundred dollars recognizing that, as a private, I did not have the money immediately available to me. He told me not to be concerned about the inspection. He knew my board was up to date, and he could handle any changes that would come through in my absence. I was able to make it to Knoxville, walk in and surprise Mom at the hospital that Saturday evening. Mom's surgery and recovery went well, and I returned to my unit in Maine.

When I returned, Lantis called me into his office and asked: "How would you like to go to Vietnam?" Thinking he was kidding, I said: "Sure, can I leave tomorrow?" Then I realized his comment was a serious one.

This is when God set things into motion. I never received a promotion while at Loring; however, it later came under very unique circumstances. Because of my performance reviews, I was among seven soldiers nominated from our home base in Fort Devens, Massachusetts. The nomination was for one position, a prestigious assignment with the Military Assistance Command, Vietnam (MACV). This was in the spring of 1965 and before the first U.S. military divisions were assigned to Vietnam. It was for an administrative position with a MACV advisory team. This was a big deal. Those receiving such assignments had to have a FBI background check for a U.S. Department of Defense "Secret" security clearance. Of the seven nominated, I was selected.

My trip to Vietnam began with a conversation with God. As the chartered commercial Trans World Airlines Boeing 707 taxied down the runway at California's Travis Air Force Base, my thoughts turned to God. I prayed: "I am on my way to a war zone. If it is Your wish that I return safe and sound, I can accept that. If it is Your wish that I not return, I am also prepared for that eventuality as well. I place myself in Your hands." As soon as my thoughts ended, I felt a sensation from my head going through my entire body. That sensation included a level of calm, so much so, that even the sound of the jet engines and the roar of the plane speeding down the runway were silent for that brief period. God had immediately responded to my message to Him. From that point on, I approached my upcoming tour of duty in Vietnam with the upmost confidence.

When I arrived in Vietnam in August 1965, I was still eighteen years old and would be the youngest soldier assigned to my advisory team.

The tour began with two weeks of orientation at Military Assistance Command, Vietnam Headquarters in Saigon, Vietnam. The two week program ended with a briefing and pep talk from none other than Four-Star General William Westmoreland. There were only about 20 soldiers in this small conference room and to have an opportunity to be briefed by someone who was a celebrity back home was indeed a special moment for me. General Westmoreland was commander of all the troops in Vietnam at the time. Upon receiving our assignments, I was dispatched to Vinh Binh Province in the Mekong Delta where MACV Advisory Team #57 was headquartered. The town was Phu Vinh and was also called Tra Vinh depending on which map was used as a reference.

My new unit was headed by a senior advisor, Lt. Col. Frank H. Duggins, Jr. Apparently, MACV Headquarters had processed my papers upon my arrival in Saigon and realized I was still a PFC. In September, MACV issued orders for my promotion to E-4. Duggins, realizing that he had not requested my promotion, the orders were sent back to Saigon based on what was perceived to be a mistake. The orders were returned and he was advised to promote me, because the original order already had an effective date and would not be rescinded. Six months later, Duggins submitted a request for early promotion for me to sergeant E-5 and it was granted in June 1966. I had been in Vietnam less than 10 months and had received two promotions. Even more amazing was that I received the E-5 rank right at two years of total military service.

Was my lack of promotion while at Loring AFB an act of racism? I don't know. However, in the final analysis, it didn't really matter.

Our team consisted of a cadre of headquarters support personnel including administration and supply. We had five subsector teams assigned to local districts throughout the province. These subsector teams were direct advisors to the Vietnamese military units. They consisted of a subsector team advisor, normally a major; a junior officer, usually a captain with an artillery background; and two infantry noncommissioned officers, a medic and radio operator.

Our headquarters were in two former French villas. One was used for an office which was across the street. The other villa was an all-purpose building, which also served as a barracks. It was located in a gated compound. At the time of my arrival there was one other building inside the compound which served as a warehouse, mess hall, and sleeping quarters. All of these facilities were in the middle of the town of Phu Vinh. The location offered a degree of security in that the town served as somewhat of a buffer zone against an assault on our facilities.

As the team expanded, a new barracks was constructed in the compound and all of the junior grade enlisted men were assigned to those quarters. The expansion was not necessarily for new advisory team members, but for a United States Air Force medical team that was assigned to support the local Vietnamese hospital. There were two physicians and a number of medical technicians. Our role was to provide security and housing. In addition to the Air Force medical personnel, there were three civilian female nurses who had voluntarily come to Vietnam, to join them as a part of a humanitarian mission. They lived in a separate villa a block from our compound.

Vinh Binh Province was actually a peninsula bordered by the South China Sea to the east and the Bassac and Son Co Chien Rivers south and north respectively. These rivers were tributaries of the famous Mekong River and presented many challenges for our unit. The Viet Cong would use the river system and the related canals to travel from one province to the next. This made it difficult to keep up with how many enemy soldiers may be located in our province at any given time.

To minimize the potential of a massive Viet Cong build-up in our province, our advisory team was assigned two O-1 Birddog aircraft to fly multiple daily observation missions, to look out for any unusual movements along the rivers and canals. One was a U.S. Army plane and the other was flown by a U.S. Air Force pilot. Coincidentally, the Army pilot was Lt. Hal Collins, call sign "Shotgun 15", who was born and raised in Spring City, Tennessee, which is about a 45-minute drive from Knoxville. Lt Collins subscribed to the *Knoxville News Sentinel* newspaper and would share them with me.

In addition to flying observer missions, the Air Force pilot had another very important role, Forward Air Control. The FAC pilot would direct the U.S. Air Force and Vietnam Air Force fighter planes in placing their payload (bombs). They would be on the scene during a specific rendezvous time to place one of the four smoke rockets housed in pods on the wings of the O-1 Birddog. The rockets provided a large puff of white smoke that the fighter pilots used as their target. The other mission of these pilots was to serve as escorts for our convoys travelling along the roads of the delta. They were a safety net, eyes in the sky so to speak, in the event of an enemy attack on the personnel traveling below.

I enjoyed a great relationship with the pilots and their crew chiefs. The O-1 Birddog was a Cessna two-seat single engine plane. It begged the question, why on most occasions did these pilots fly solo when the rear seat was available? Most weekends were boring to say the least. One Saturday afternoon, I noticed Collins preparing to head to the airfield to take-off on one of his observation missions. I approached him and asked if he wanted some company. Shockingly, he said sure, get your rifle and bullet-proof vest and hop in the jeep. (I could now add official observer to my adventures in Vietnam.) Having discovered that I enjoyed flying with the pilots, one weekend Air Force Capt. Shumate, call sign "Bart 103," invited me to fly with him to put in a bomb strike with some U.S. Air Force F-4s at Duyen Hai District bordering the South China Sea. This was an exciting opportunity. I was able to take my Super 8mm home movie camera and shoot the whole thing from the air. The only dangerous part of the mission was that Shumate purposely arrived at the predetermined target site ten minutes early. His goal was to fly over the area at tree top level to see if he could draw fire from the enemy below. Receiving hostile fire would give him a more precise place to direct the fighter jets when they arrived. We received hostile fire on our first pass, confirming the enemy presence. The enemy did not know that in about 10 minutes Captain Shumate had a surprise for them. This footage is edited with that from other flights and is a part of my home movie library.

My military job classification was still clerk typist specialist. Our office clerical support allocation consisted of an E-5 administrative specialist and two clerk typists. When I arrived at my office in Vietnam, there was an E-5 administrative specialist and I was the only clerk typist. The E-5 gave me an overview of the duties as, well as all of the reports that were due to our division headquarters in nearby Vinh Long Province and the submission schedules. These reports were consolidated and forwarded on to MACV Headquarters in Saigon. He did a great job in giving me a crash course on these issues. I later discovered that the reason for the crash course was that he was transferring back to the States in three weeks. This left me, a clerk typist, with no administrative specialist oversight or the much needed second authorized clerk typist for our unit.

My immediate supervisor became Lt. Col. Frank H. Duggins Jr. He arrived in Vietnam two weeks before I did and had been assigned as senior advisor to the Vinh Binh Province Chief, who was a Vietnamese military lieutenant colonel. The best way to describe our relationship is that I was to Colonel Duggins what Radar was to Colonel Potter on the *M*A*S*H* television series. There were other similarities to this television show and our unit. We were isolated from any major military installations, and we were on our on with very little to do to relieve the boredom.

After being advised to promote me, I think Duggins gained some immediate confidence in my abilities. I would work long hours during the periods when the end of the month reports were due. Since we were shorthanded, I had to manage my workload very stringently. I gave the five officers who had to file reports specific deadlines to have them to me for typing and processing. I would then be responsible for them being dispatched to division. On one occasion, a ranking officer tested my system by submitting his draft a day late. I immediately informed him that there were no guarantees his report would make schedule. At the time I was working on a report that a lower ranking officer had submitted on time. The major immediately felt that rank had its privileges and marched me into Duggins' office for a confrontation. Upon hearing his appeal and telling Duggins that I was being insubordinate, I reminded Duggins of my system and told him that the major was a day late getting his report to me and I chose not to delay the junior officer's report. This major did not know I had another ace up my sleeve. This is when I mentioned to Duggins how disappointed I was going back to the compound after working late and finding the major playing cards with him and two other officers. I was immediately excused from the meeting, and the next thing I knew the major was sitting at a typewriter across from me typing his own report. Upon completing the junior officer's report, I turned to the major and offered to complete his report. He gladly accepted my offer. Both reports made the schedule. I did not want any delay to reflect upon the colonel.

At some point, MACV decided to assign a captain with an administrative background to our unit. Here I am short both an E-5 administrative specialist and an E-4 clerk typist, and now have to cope with Captain Byrnes who had very little to contribute as my new supervisor.

Noticing that my filing was behind, he decided to approach the colonel, in my presence, to tell him that he would like to request an E-5 administrative specialist to support me in the office. I was still an E-4 at the time. Duggins's immediate response was: "I have an administrative specialist, and I suggest you requisition Specialist Bussell some clerical assistance." The next words uttered from the captain was: "But Colonel. . . ". Before he could complete his sentence, Duggins responded: "Captain, in this man's army, when a captain addresses a colonel, there are no buts."

The colonel frequently recognized my contribution to the advisory team's mission. I volunteered to visit the local Catholic orphanage and take treats to the kids. This included participating in a clothing drive soliciting children's clothing from our families back home. In addition, the team paid me $35 a month to run the projector for the evening movies when they were made available. Occasionally, Army Special Services would send a Disney-type film, and I would load up the projection equipment and take it to the orphanage to show the kids the movie outside under the stars. I usually ended up with a couple of the kids falling asleep on my lap. I spent my spare time being as productive as possible. We had a radio operator who was responsible for monitoring all communications throughout the day. He would be relieved in the evening by the personnel assigned in charge of quarters. As with the clerical situation, we were short two radio operators. There was no better place to write letters back home than to sit in the radio shack and keep company with S.Sgt. Comier. There was generally not a lot of radio traffic, unless a combat operation was in progress. Because of my interest in learning the functions of a radio operator, S.Sgt. Comier worked with me on the protocol. He gave me a copy of the phonetic alphabet— Alpha, Bravo, Charlie... —to learn. He then supervised me until he felt I was ready to actually handle radio transmissions, even showing me how to break the radios down and clean them. One day he turned to me and said: "I am going to take a break. You've got the radio."

Becoming a proficient Intermediate Speed (IS) Radio operator afforded me some new and different adventures. During operations, I would serve as Duggins's radio operator at the field command post.

His call sign was Cascade 6. As his radio operator, I became Cascade 6 Alpha. The command post was generally set-up at the Phu Vinh airfield. The mission was monitored there because of the activity associated with the helicopter gunships flying in and out for refueling. The command post was also there to ensure that support was readily available to the units during the operation to include calling in air support from fighter jets, should the situation arise.

Speaking of the helicopters needing refueling, there were times outside of combat operations when helicopters were incoming and needed to be refueled. On one of these occasions, the sergeant who normally drove the fuel truck was not available. I found myself driving the fuel truck from the compound to the airfield. This was about a one-mile trip. We would always have an escort jeep travel in front of the fuel truck due to its size and the crowded narrow roads. The jeep would head to the airfield with horn blasting to clear a path for the truck. I had driven the lead jeep for the fuel truck in the past, and on this particular occasion I was bold enough to take on the fuel truck with another soldier driving the escort vehicle. This is how I spent my weekends avoiding boredom. Many of the guys found the bar more appealing and a number of them turned to alcohol as a way of coping in the combat zone.

The colonel used these details as a part of his justification to recommend me for early promotion to sergeant E-5. The promotion was approved as specialist 5th class due to administrative nature of my job. (Note: The army eventually eliminated the specialist 5th class designation and reverted back to sergeant E-5.)

Later in my tour, I convinced Duggins to allow me to accompany Captain Al Fuimano as his radio operator on one of the combat operations. My argument was I was in great physical shape and it would be a shame to spend a year in Vietnam and never experience walking through the rice paddies that were so prevalent in the Mekong Delta. And yes, we did have to walk in waist deep water in the paddies themselves because the dikes surrounding them would oftentimes have land mines, and only the rice farmers knew where they were located. On the occasion of this day-long mission with Fuimano, we spotted three Viet Cong in an adjacent rice field as they were fleeing to avoid contact with us.

This was fairly typical for these operations. As we would enter villages covered by the scope of the operation, there would be only women and children. The men and older boys were nowhere to be found. On a number of occasions at the end of the operation, after all the villages had been swept, the observer pilots would see the men and boys returning.

The Viet Cong engagement of choice was to hit and run. Establishing ambushes around road mines were very common, and we had to take extra precautions as we traveled through the province. Oftentimes the Vietnamese locals would make us aware of ambush threats in the area. They had a vested interest, in that we were accompanied by Vietnamese soldiers who were likely their relatives. The Viet Cong would also use mortar attacks on the town; however, the closest they seemed to get to our compound was the equivalent of three or four blocks.

Another one of the coincidences I experienced was in April 1966. The United States authorized the first B-52 Bomber raid in the Mekong Delta. The site selected was none other than the Duyen Hai District, in Vinh Binh Province. This was the Viet Cong stronghold near the South China Sea, and the only district in the province where we did not have a subsector team. One of the ironies of this mission was that prior to my assignment in Vietnam, I was stationed at Loring Air Force Base, Maine. This was an Air Force Strategic Air Command (SAC) B-52 base. Having spent nine months seeing the B-52s take-off and land, I found myself almost a year later in an area where you could actually feel the ground rumble from the impact of their bombs. The B-52s were six miles up in the air when they dropped their load. Our unit had provided the coordinates for the strike and Bart 103 was in the area to observe. While serving as FAC for the fighter jets, Bart 103 had radio contact with them. The B-52 aircrafts for this mission were part of the Strategic Air Command based in Guam. Because of this, Bart 103 did not have any radio contact with the B-52 bomber pilots.

As part of the bombing mission, our advisory team had set into motion a ground operation to go into the area to assess the damage following the raid. This operation reported two hundred VC killed in what was, at that time, the largest claim of the war for a single raid.

As June 1966 approached, I was in the tenth month of my twelve-month tour of duty in Vietnam. I received orders for my next assignment. I was scheduled to report to an special operations unit at Fort Bragg, North Carolina. Being one year out from completing my three-year enlistment, a number of factors lead me to make an unusual decision.

The first, was that a couple of our guys had left our advisory team and transferred to Fort Campbell, Kentucky, or Fort Benning, Georgia and found themselves back in Vietnam in three months, when their newly assigned unit was deployed. Secondly, serving in a combat zone had its financial rewards. In addition to my base pay of $365 per month, I received stipends for foreign duty, hostile fire combat pay, cost-of-living allowance, and a subsistence allowance. These allowances added about $250 per month to my pay. I had a joint savings account with Mom back home. I received a $100 a month and the Army direct-deposited a little over $500 into the savings account each month. It served as a means for me to support Mom and the family back home. This was one of my goals in enlisting in the Army. This money was all tax free. Finally, I had not decided whether or not I would become a career soldier.

With those things in mind, I discussed with the colonel the idea of extending my tour with Advisory Team #57 for another six months. He approved my request and submitted it through channels. In the meantime, Duggins had received his new assignment, which was to become Commandant for the Department of Army's, U.S. Military Academy Preparatory School at Fort Belvoir, Virginia.

Either way, I would no longer have my principal source of support and encouragement. Colonel Duggins was like a father figure to me. I learned a lot of life's lessons under his mentorship, the most important being how to become a leader and gain the respect of subordinates. It was common knowledge in MACV circles that Advisory Team #57 was one of the elite units. Other combat support units that were called on to interface with our team always appreciated how organized and well-planned our combat operations were. On one occasion, an American helicopter from our division headquarters in Vinh Long was shot down during a monsoon storm that hit in the middle of the operation. Shotgun 15 and the other helicopters flew over the crash site and realized that none of the crew were able to escape and were killed in action.

The natural reaction of the helicopter team leader was to come back to the airfield, refuel, and return to retrieve his comrades. Duggins made it over to the team leader as soon as he landed. He informed the helicopter team that darkness was about to fall and that there would be no attempt to retrieve the crew today. He then put his arms around the distraught pilot and told him that our team had made arrangements to secure the airfield and that we had accommodations for him and his crew at our compound to spend the night. The colonel had already coordinated this with the lead pilot's command in Vinh Long before the helicopter unit returned to our airfield.

Duggins's goal was to sit down and plan a recovery strategy for the next day. He ordered air force fighter strikes to soften up the target area, medivac helicopters and a chinook helicopter with a crane to air-lift the wreckage. The operation went off without a problem. The lead pilot indicated that Duggins was an outstanding commander and it was an honor to provide support for our team. In this instance, Colonel Duggins revealed his compassionate spirit.

Before Duggins departed in August 1966, he had recommended me for the Bronze Star Medal. It was a proud moment for the both of us when he presented it to me. The colonel left Advisory Team #57 after a year and we had no American assigned to our team killed in action under his leadership. Being with the team made me feel secure in my decision to stay another six months.

My relationship with the colonel did not end with his departure. Upon arriving at his new assignment, he sent me a letter with a copy of the army regulation and application for me to come to the preparatory school. As a West Point graduate himself, he wanted me to complete the two years of study there and move on to the West Point Military Academy. I did not have an interest, and wasn't confident that I had the academic background to compete in this type of class work, because I had avoided all of the college preparatory math and science courses in high school. At the time, I had no plans to attend college and did not think they were necessary.

One of the perks of extending my tour for six months was that I had the option of taking a thirty-day leave, giving me the opportunity to return to the States for a visit. I exercised this option; however, I did not tell Mom that I was coming home. From the day I arrived in Vietnam, I made it a point to write her a letter every day as a way of easing her from worrying about me. I would send pictures of me playing basketball with some of the guys in the compound and shielded her from my many escapades. Sometimes our airfield would go two or three days without getting a supply aircraft which would also pick up our outgoing mail. Therefore, Mom would get two or three letters arriving in Knoxville at the same time.

It was now August 1966 and with the leave approved, I had to sign a waiver that if free space on military transportation was not available, I had the funds to defray the commercial airline cost to and from Saigon. Arriving at Ton Son Nhut Airbase, I signed up for a military chartered commercial flight to Travis Air Force Base in California. Some of the incoming soldiers made those of us returning to the States aware that there was a major airline strike and that Delta was the only major airline flying. Delta Air Lines was a nonunion carrier at that time and was not impacted by the nationwide airline machinist union strike. With this being the case, it would make it difficult to get from the west coast to Knoxville. The last flight departed Ton Son Nhut at midnight. Two other soldiers and I did not make the cut. This meant spending the night in Saigon and trying our luck the next day.

But God had plans for me. Upon returning to the military dispatch counter, we informed the desk sergeant that we did not make the last flight and we wanted to be placed on the next day's list. The desk sergeant had a thought. He had one of his subordinates put us on a truck that took us over to the military cargo side of the airfield, with the hopes that we could catch a cargo plane. When we arrived, the desk sergeant told us he had an Air Force C-141 enroute and it would be making a return trip to the States later that morning. This was about 1:00 a.m. when we had this conversation. When the C-141 landed, the pilots told us to be prepared for a 4:00 a.m. departure. The C-141 StarLifter, as it was called, was developed under the late President Kennedy and unveiled in August 1963. It was the first all-jet military troop and cargo carrier and was placed in service in 1965. The C-141's speed proved invaluable during the Vietnam War by cutting roundtrip flight time between California and Saigon from 95 to 34 hours. It was built by Lockheed at their Marietta, Georgia facility.

The story gets better and divine intervention played a large part in what was about to unfold. We took-off on schedule. The C-141 StarLifter was virtually empty. After a brief stop at a U.S. Air Force

Base in Yokota, Japan, we proceeded on to a refueling stop at an air force base in Anchorage, Alaska. Acknowledging the airline strike in the United States, I asked the pilot about his estimated time of arrival at Travis Air Force Base. He asked me where I was headed. I told him Knoxville. This is when he informed me that he wasn't going to Travis; he was leaving Anchorage and headed to Charleston Air Force Base in South Carolina. I told him that I could walk to Knoxville from there.

God's intervention did not stop there. Delta Airlines had excellent service throughout the Southeastern part of the United States. When I arrived at the Delta ticket counter in Charleston, the ticket agent informed me that the early morning flight to Atlanta was booked from Columbia, South Carolina, which was its next stop. She would only sell me a ticket from Charleston to Columbia. At least that placed me closer to Knoxville. Taking off from Charleston, as soon as we were airborne the pilot came on the intercom and said that he had some bad news. He indicated that Columbia was fogged in and he was pro-ceeding on to Atlanta. The guy who only paid for the price of a ticket to Columbia wasn't complaining about being taken all the way to Atlanta.

Once in Atlanta, Delta had five or six flights a day going to and from Knoxville. I was able to get a military standby ticket on the first flight. Once in Knoxville, I caught a taxi from the airport to Mom's house. The big surprise was now in its final stage. Arriving in my neighborhood, I spotted my uncle, Booker Berry, sitting on his front porch.

At the time, I did not realize that Mom was inside his home vis-iting with her twin sister, my aunt Margaret. Uncle Booker apparently opened the front door and said: "Louise, I think I just saw Jimmy riding down the street in a taxi." Although our house was on the next block, the rear lot of the two houses were connected. Mom peered out their back window and sure enough saw a taxi in front of her house. The next thing I noticed was this fifty-three-year-old woman running through her backyard and down the driveway like a track star to greet her son. It had been over a year since I departed for Vietnam and it was good to be back in familiar territory. While she was happy to see me, I waited until the next day to tell her that after about 26 days, I would be heading back to my unit in the Mekong Delta.

Overall, it was a good time. It was great being around family and friends. What made an impression on me was the progress that was being made on the employment front for some of the neighborhood guys and my former high school classmates. One of my reasons for joining the army was a lack of employment opportunities for African-Americans. With the passage of the 1964 Civil Rights Act, the positive impact was being felt by the African-American community. Many of the high school graduates were now employed with firms like the Alcoa Aluminum Plant, the Tennessee Valley Authority, and Union Carbide which at the time was operating the Atomic Energy Commission Y-12 Plant, birthplace of the atomic bomb, in neighboring Oak Ridge. This trip home provided me with new found insight regarding the job market and presented a new alternative to becoming a career soldier. This was the most productive aspect of my trip home.

What was most impressive was that many of my friends were now driving new muscle cars which had become a trend in America. Of all the cars I saw while at home, the 1966 Pontiac GTO impressed me the most.

In my return to Vietnam, I traveled back to Charleston Air Force Base. The C-141 pilot encouraged me to come back to Charleston when I was ready to return to Vietnam. He said they had a number of weekly flights going directly back to Vietnam which would enable me to fly back on the Air Force's dime. He presented me with a business card to introduce myself to the dispatchers at Charleston AFB for assistance in getting back to Vietnam.

Upon arriving, I discovered there were no flights scheduled for Vietnam for a couple of days. While there was an attempt to get me on a special embassy flight, which was departing for Vietnam the next day, I did not have a passport. As it was explained to me, the embassy flight was going to Vietnam; however, it was going to take about five days. This was because the flight was leaving Charleston and headed first for embassies in Europe, and would end up in Vietnam after traveling halfway around the world in an eastern direction.

The dispatch sergeant decided that to get around the passport issue, they could cut orders to make me an official messenger. This would allow me access to the flight; however, I would be restricted to the bases to which we traveled. That was fine with me and I did not see a problem with me reporting two or three days late to my unit.

The only thing required was the signature of the duty officer, a first lieutenant Women Air Force (WAF) officer. She did not go along with the plan and refused to sign the documentation. I don't normally play the race card; however, in this case I sensed that it was applicable.

The dispatch sergeant then told me that he could not get me back to Vietnam, but he could place me on a flight they had going to Travis Air Force Base. Later that day, I boarded a C-130 cargo plane headed for California. Arriving at Travis AFB, I was able to get a military transport back to Vietnam without having the expense of flying commercial.

Returning back to Advisory Team #57, I received updates from the administrative specialist who was on loan from division headquarters in Vinh Long in my absence. I am now reporting to Lt. Col. Lawrence Bulawsky, who was a little more laid back than Duggins, and with whom I quickly developed an excellent working relationship. He told me that when he was processing through division headquarters, his superiors told him I was the most knowledgeable person on the team. They told Bulawsky that their officers relied heavily on me for information and that he could certainly benefit from my understanding of the workings of the unit. That was both very encouraging and refreshing to hear.

Midway through my six months' extension, the safety and security that had been our history under Duggins was rocked. On November 13, 1966, a convoy with Vietnamese Captain Ba, (district chief), his American counterpart Major Ernest E. Layaou Jr., (subsector advisor) and medic Sgt. James D. Tyner departed Cang Long District Town to investigate a road mined by the Viet Cong the previous night. Reports were that the unit was warned of a possible ambush by some of the villagers. Our team and the district chief ordered heavy artillery fire in the area where the road mine was placed. This was a customary practice. The Viet Cong were obviously prepared and dug in sufficiently enough that they were not hit by the artillery barrage.

The Viet Cong had set up an elaborate ambush at the road mining site. The ambush killed both Layaou and Tyner. They were the first American team members killed in action in my 15-plus months with the team. In response to the deaths of these team members, Sergeant First Class Corpus from team headquarters volunteered to take an assignment with the Cang Long subsector team until Tyner could be replaced. Another soldier who had just reported to the unit, S.Sgt. Green, who was waiting assignment to a subsector team, was also dispatched to shore up the team. Major Layaou was replaced by his second in command, Capt. Tremayne.

Three weeks later on December 6, the Viet Cong established a road block in the Cang Long District. A response team was sent out which included Tremayne, Corpus and Green along with radio operator, Specialist Custer. In an eerie turn of events, the team was also ambushed resulting in Green's death. (I recently learned by checking the web site that tracks former members of MACV Advisory Team #57, that then Major Tremayne was killed in action in April 1967, a month after my March 1967 departure.)

The most difficult thing for me was the responsibility for typing up what the military referred to as a Memo for Record, also known as an After Action Report, outlining the sequence of events. The report was an actual timeline of the attack and the response.

These incidents called for a full-fledged response, especially when American lives were at risk. In both cases, helicopter gunship support and Air Force jet fighters were called in with Bart 103 and Shotgun 15 coordinating things from the air. In both incidents, the Medevac helicopters transported the American KIA directly to the military morgue in Saigon to prepare them for their return to the States.

Each incident was followed by a memorial service for our fallen comrades at our headquarters in Vinh Binh. A military chaplain was flown in on both occasions. An African-American captain, Louis Boston, took the responsibility of organizing the service on our end. Boston was an aspiring minister and God would later allow him to play a significant part in my life.

The balance of my tour was uneventful. After extending my tour in Vietnam, I subsequently decided not to reenlist at the end of my three-year obligation. The Army notified me that rather than assign me to another base for the ninety days remaining on my enlistment, they were going to give me an early out discharge. This meant my departure date of March 10, 1967, would be my last official assignment. I would travel to Travis AFB, and then on to the Oakland, California Army Terminal for discharge.

In preparation for my end of tour, I had a local Vietnamese carpenter build me a wooden box in which to ship my belongings back to the States. They generally asked that you ship baggage three weeks prior to your scheduled departure. I also made a trip to Saigon three weeks out. While there, I went to the office of the General Motors Corp.'s foreign sales representative. All of the U.S. automobile man-ufactures had representatives which would allow American soldiers to order new cars directly from their factory. The soldiers could cus-tomize their car by selecting specific options and receive factory pricing without dealer markups. These cars would then be shipped to the stateside dealer of our choice. I ordered a 1967 Tyrol Blue Pontiac GTO with a black vinyl top. We were only required to pay the repre-sentative a $100 commission with overall financing arranged when the car was delivered to our respective towns.

Lt. Col. Bulawsky had recommended me for the U.S. Army Commendation Medal which was approved. He presented it to me prior to my departure. This was a nice addition to the Bronze Star Medal I had received under Duggins.

Reflecting on my tour of duty in Vietnam, there were a number of highlights and coincidences. One that deserves mention is the encounter I had with Maj. Archie Bassham, a Caucasian and a native of Alabama. His tour was ending, and he asked me to type a personal letter for him addressed to his Vietnamese counterpart. I typed the letter and presented it to him. He reached into his wallet and pulled out a ten dollar bill to pay me. I told him that friends do not charge friends to do favors. To my amazement, he paused, with wallet still in hand, as a tear streamed down his cheek. I took a step back, saluted him and told him, sir, have a safe trip home. I have an idea what that tear represented. My thoughts went back to my experience with the Alabama National Guardsmen back at Fort Jackson. God had allowed me to touch the heart of a person who could now look beyond my color.

My other highlights included the support of the United Service Organization. The USO provides entertainment for troops at military bases overseas. One way of accomplishing their mission was to pro-mote the visit of celebrities. During my stint in Vietnam, I had the opportunity to interact with the likes of baseball stars Henry Aaron, Joe Torre, Brooks Robinson, and Stan Musial, as well as the broad-caster Mel Allen, all of whom toured together. Members of the 1965 Los Angeles Lakers—Rudy LaRusso, Darrell Immhoff, and LeRoy Ellis also visited our base, and I even got a chance to play against them in a pick-up game. My favorite visiting entertainers were comedienne Martha Raye and Hugh O'Brien, who as a kid I had watched as Wyatt

Earp on television. O'Brien actually came in as his Wyatt Earp character complete with his six-gun and holster.

Another one of those unusual coincidences orchestrated by God was the visit of actor Robert Mitchum. In 1958, Mitchum produced, co-wrote, and starred in a movie called *Thunder Road,* based on the moonshining trade in my native Harlan County, Kentucky. The movie chronicled how the bootleggers drove supped-up cars to outrun federal and local law enforcement. Mitchum played the most prominent bootlegger, who was not only evading the law, but carpetbag bootleggers who wanted to take over his family's territory. The movie ended with a chase scene that went from Kentucky all the way to Knoxville. It concluded with Mitchum's character dying in a crash right outside of Bearden, less than two miles from my Knoxville neighborhood. Mitchum is also credited with co-writing the theme song for the movie, *The Ballad of Thunder Road.* Again, what are the odds?

My departure from Vietnam ended on a very humorous note. The U.S. Department of Defense had contracts with American commercial airlines to fly troops to and from Vietnam. One of the contracts was with Braniff International Airlines, which was noted for its fifteen different exterior color schemes on its aircraft. They actually sent a pink airplane to Vietnam to fly my group back to the States. While on the tarmac waiting for instructions to take-off from Ben Hua Air Force Base, a stewardess came out of the cockpit laughing. While in there with the pilots, she overheard the military air traffic controller telling her Braniff crew: "Okay, sweetie you can take off now."

This was the end of a great adventure. As we taxied down the runway, I thanked God for protecting me. My mind immediately drifted to thoughts of what God had in store. He obviously saved me for a purpose.

Army Basic Training on bivouac (camping) and field exercises.

Specialist Fourth Class Bussell as his desk in Vietnam (1965)

Specialist Fifth Class Bussell receiving map reading instructions from
Major Harold Luck (1966)

Driving fuel truck at Phu Vinh Airfield, Vietnam (1966)

Actor Hugh O'Brien (television's Wyatt Earp) visit Advisory Team #57 with six-shooter. Colonel Duggins is to O'Brien's left (1966)

Los Angeles Laker basketball great Leroy Ellis
visits Advisory Team #57 (1966)

Advisory Team #57 Group Photo (including civilian nurses on humanitarian mission at local Vietnamese hospital)

My 1967 Pontiac G.T.O.

Transition from Military to Civilian Life

U pon being discharged at the Oakland, California Army Terminal, I caught the first available flight to Knoxville. It was March 10, 1967. Not knowing what was waiting for me, I left the military with the option of reenlisting within 60 days without losing my E-5 rank. Keep in mind, I had enlisted at seventeen, and I was leaving at twenty years old, my military obligation behind me. When I was being discharged, I was informed that I had to report to my local selective service board to update my draft status so that I would not be sent a draft notice in the future. While at the selective service office I ran into one of my high school classmates. I remember being teased the final two weeks of high school regarding my choice of enlisting in the military. Classmates would call out the military cadence when I walked down the halls. This particular classmate received a classification of 1A which meant that he was expected to be drafted immediately. He had apparently forgotten that I had enlisted immediately following our graduation and asked me how I was classified. I told him that I was "B". He looked on the form and determined that there was no classification "B". This is when I informed him that: "I will be here when you leave and be here when you get back." Given his status, that was probably a mean thing to say; however, I couldn't resist.

When I returned home, my initial goal was to rest for a few days and wait for my new Pontiac GTO to arrive. After the first week, I began the process of applying for jobs with some of the governmental agencies and their contractors. With my veteran's preference, I felt this was my best option. I also applied at private sector companies like Alcoa Aluminum. The Tennessee Valley Authority reviewed my application and invited me to take their clerical test battery. Having an administrative background in the military, I scored well on their test and my typing skills also came in handy.

My GTO arrived after two weeks. I would spend the mornings applying for work and the afternoons cruising the two college campuses—historically black Knoxville College and the University of Tennessee. One of the drawbacks of being twenty years old and a military vet was that the neighborhood fathers did not want me near their daughters. Despite the fact that their eighteen-year-old high school senior daughters were only two years younger than me, I was not to be trusted. On one occasion, I finally got an OK to take out a girl that I liked before I enlisted. I excitedly pulled into her driveway, rang the doorbell, and was greeted by my date and her fifteen-year-old sister, who apparently had become a part of the date package. I wish I can tell you that the three of us had a great time, but I can't. Time to head into another direction.

With my sixty-day window for reenlistment beginning to close, I received a job offer from TVA. I spoke with Ed Butler, the employment officer for my appointment, who gave me a date and time to report for employment processing. My employment effective date was April 26, 1967. On my reporting date, Butler told me that I was being assigned to a TVA construction site in Lenoir City, Tennessee, which was about a 35 mile drive from my home in west Knoxville. The job was with TVA's Division of Construction's Tellico Dam Project which was in its start-up phase. What I found strange about the discussion I had with Butler, was that he placed a lot of emphasis on my background and told me that he did not expect me to go down there and screw-up. He was seemly attempting to prepare me for something that was unique about my hire. I later learned why all of this preparatory discussion was necessary.

After I had been at Tellico for a few weeks, I had to travel to the Division of Construction headquarters in downtown Knoxville. While there, I decided to visit Butler. This is when he informed me that I was the first African-American to work in a TVA construction office. He laughed when he told me that when I arrived on site and reported to my supervisor, Ed Bryant, he had walked to the other end of our office trailer and called Butler. Bryant's first words were: "You did not tell me that James was a Negro. We are not ready for a Negro in a construction office." To which Butler responded: That's why I didn't tell you, because I knew that would be your reaction. Butler informed him that he was stuck with me because I was the most qualified candidate in the clerical pool. Bryant's concern was not personal, but based on the fact that as payroll clerk and time checker, I would have to spend a good deal of time in the field with the unionized skill trade workers. The unions, in this area, were not yet integrated and he did not know how I would be received. I would like to add that Bryant became a great mentor for me. He knew TVA policy and procedures and would take the time to share information that would allow me to get ahead. He also passed excellent reports, regarding my performance, up the chain-of-command to the Division of Construction's top management.

There are ironies associated with my assignment at the Tellico Dam Construction Project. Tellico Dam was constructed on "Bussell Island." Folks, I can't make this stuff up. I was told by some of the locals, that at one time, there was a "Bussell Ferry" that transported people and goods across the Tennessee River in that area. I don't understand why they didn't just go ahead and name the facility, "Bussell Dam". It would have been appropriate.

This assignment set the tone for what my relationship was going to be with TVA for years to come. As I began my interaction with the workers on the job, God allowed me to use humor when confronted with three white workers on my first trip to the field. As payroll clerk, it was my job to take the weekly checks to the workers. Not realizing at the time that I was the first African-American to hold such a position at a TVA Construction site, and being the only one on the payroll, this turned out to be a new experience for the workers there, as well. Upon getting out of the TVA vehicle, I spotted three pile driver crew members standing next to a fire barrel keeping warm right above the Little Tennessee River. The Tellico Dam project was actually designed to dam the Little Tennessee River to transition it to become Tellico Lake. As I approached, I noticed one man nudge the other standing next to him. My immediate thoughts were that this is going to be my first challenge. I presented the first two workers their checks and the one that I had observed doing the nudging spat on the ground and asked: "Hey boy, can you tap dance and shuffle like that Sammy Davis boy I saw on television last night?" Without a word, I took two steps, dangled his check over the Little Tennessee and asked him: "Can you swim like Johnny Weissmuller?" (Weissmuller was an Olympic Gold Medal swimmer who went on to play Tarzan on television and in the movies.) The other two workers started laughing and one said: "John I bet you'll leave that boy alone now." John looked at me and said: "Give me my check, son. You are going to be alright." This turned out to be a defining moment for me. I am sure they expected me to react by quitting and going home. Since I had passed their initiation, John became my biggest advocate on the construction site. I was told he would alert new workers that I was off limits and anyone who gave me a hard time would have to deal with him and his fellow pile drivers.

There was an occasion where one of the new guys did not get the memo regarding me being off limits. As I walked into one of the labor shacks to pay some of the men, who were on their lunch break, a recently hired laborer asked me if I wanted to see his Ku Klux Klan membership card. I asked him if he wanted to see my Black Panther membership card. I added that while the KKK was burning crosses, we almost burned down the City of Detroit last week. Another one learned that I was not intimidated.

One of my counterparts at the Division of Construction's central payroll office in Knoxville was a guy by the name of William Brice, who was an older U.S. Air Force veteran. After about a year with TVA, Brice told me that he and a number of African-American veterans were enrolled in night school at UT. He said it was something I might want to consider.

I did follow through with Brice's invitation and began taking a course at UT's evening school Fall Quarter 1968. My first course was English Composition 101, a freshman prerequisite, and I made a C in the course. It was an hour and half on Monday and Wednesday nights for three hours credit. During the Winter Quarter, I got ambitious and decided to take English Composition 102 and two additional three hour courses, one on Tuesday and the other on Thursday night. The English course was still split between Monday and Wednesday. Taking nine hours and working full time took its toll on me. While I maintained my C average, I was totally exhausted.

God intervened and gave me a push. My job at the Tellico Dam was going to be impacted by actions taken by the U.S. Congress. Unlike the TVA's power generation program, which is funded through revenue from the sale of electricity, the Tellico Dam Project relied on U.S. Congressional funding. Due to budget constraints, Congress decided to ask TVA to shut down and delay the construction of the Tellico Dam for six months.

While TVA was willing to place me in a full-time job elsewhere in their Division of Construction organization, I decided this was an opportunity for me to switch gears and go to college on a full-time basis. I notified Bryant of my decision and he passed the information up the chain. To my surprise, the Division of Construction responded by offering me a part-time job in their downtown construction accounting office.

One of the keys to this decision was the need to sell my Pontiac GTO, which was still being financed. I waited until all of this was set into motion before I notified Mom of my plans. Thinking that she would be excited that her son was finally going to college as a full-time student, I was shocked at her reaction. First of all, she knew how much I enjoyed my GTO and did not want me to sell it. Secondly, she was proud that her son had a desk job with a prestigious firm like TVA. Her pride was obviously based on her experience of African-Americans not having these types of opportunities when she was growing up. She saw these jobs as significant progress for our race. She just could not understand why someone would want to walk away from such a privilege.

The most interesting response that I received was from one of the neighborhood winos. Upon hearing my news, he pulled me off to the side and these words resonated in my mind throughout my college career. He said: "Hey Bussell, do you know that if you go over there and flunk out, you won't have a job, you won't have a car, and you won't have a degree." That level of encouragement can take you far—being facetious of course.

As it turned out, those words became my motivator. This was particularly true when I learned that some people in my community were taking bets on how long it would take me to flunk out. I did spend one quarter on academic probation due to the fact that my grade point average dropped below 2.0. This was due to a number of factors. First and foremost, my lack of academic preparation during my high school years. Secondly, I was twenty-two years old and five years removed from high school. Thirdly, I just did not know how to study. (Later in life,

I discovered that I was a sufferer of Attention Deficit, Hypertension Disorder which affected my way of reading and retaining what I had gone over during my studies.) Finally, I was a little too ambitious in that I was taking a 15-quarter hour load on campus and working 20 hours a week for TVA, although the campus was in walking distance from the TVA downtown offices. Hearing that voice, "no job, no car, and no degree," forced me to reevaluate my approach to overcoming these hurdles.

The major adjustment that I made was to go to the University of Tennessee library every night for two hours after dinner. Still living a home, Mom would have dinner ready when I got home from work. I would catch a 6:00 p.m. bus to campus and study until 9:15 p.m. I would then catch a 9:30 p.m. bus back home. This pattern helped me get ahead of my studies, making me better prepared for the testing that followed. In an effort to make my target goal of graduating Spring Quarter 1973, the last two quarters I enrolled in eighteen quarter hours and maintained my twenty-hour per week job with TVA. I was proud that I made the Dean's List both quarters with a 3.4 GPA.

What was amazing to me was the encouragement I received from the bus drivers. Recognizing what I was trying to accomplish, they would place their hands over the deposit container, which would prevent me from having to pay. Over the course of my four-year career, I got to know practically every bus driver in the system. They all treated me special and were proud when I graduated. They rightly felt that they had a part in my success.

Realizing graduation was approaching, Mom asked me when the commencement exercises were scheduled. This is when I informed her that I was going to pass on this formality and not participate. She then emphatically told me that I was going to march across that stage and she was going to be there to watch. End of discussion.

Upon graduating with a Bachelor of Science Degree in Business Administration, I was employed as a personnel officer on the TVA Division of Construction's Personnel and Labor Relations Staff. My major in college was personnel and labor relations. While in college, I worked part-time in the Division of Construction's cost accounting office. Because my major was related to personnel management, in my senior year, I was transferred to TVA's Division of Personnel's central employment office as a part-time personnel clerk. Having now graduated, I received job offers from the Division of Construction and Division of Personnel. I accepted the offer from my old Division of Construction at the M-1 management level.

This is a good time to point out the divine interventions associated with this segment of my life. William Brice, the co-worker who encouraged me to go to evening school is the older brother of Jimmy Brice who had joined the Army with me in 1964. The temporary closure of the Tellico Dam provided me with the impetus to make a change in my life and pursue a college degree on a full-time basis. I had refused to take the American College Test while in high school; however, by maintaining a C average while in night school, I was able to easily transfer to regular full-time day classes without having to take the ACT. Because of my military service, I was exempted from taking mandatory ROTC courses and was given 15 hours credit. Finally, seven years after selling it, I was able to purchase my Pontiac GTO back from a TVA engineer who had purchased it from the person I sold it to in 1969. I really believe I secured the GTO once again as a significant gesture from God, rewarding me for not placing something materialist over His plans for me.

Now that my transition from college to gainful employment was complete, Karen and I could move forward with the plan we had made to get married on June 30, 1973. The process of getting married had its own series of divine interventions.

God Became Our Wedding Planner

As ridiculous as this may sound, this title is a reality. After being discharged from the service, I would drive Mom to her worship service every Sunday morning, as she was a long standing member of Knoxville's Mount Zion Baptist Church. At the end of the service, I would wait for her parked out front in my recently purchased GTO.

It apparently caught the attention of one of the church members. While waiting for Mom one Sunday, a stranger came over to me and started giving me a lecture about dropping Mom off each Sunday and not attending church service myself. I sat there, remaining noncommittal. I asked Mom who the guy was and she said that it was Lloyd A. Lee. He was a director at the local YMCA and was also very active with the youth in the church. This was not my last encounter with Lee.

A couple years later, after having sold my car and enrolled in the University of Tennessee, I was leaving my part-time job at TVA to return to classes on campus. Walking past one of the downtown bus stops, Lee was waiting on a bus when he recognized me. The next thing I know, he was again lecturing me about not being in church and emphatically told me that he expected to see me the following Sunday. After almost two years, how can you resist that level of determination and persistence? I agreed to be at church the following Sunday.

Since public transportation had become my source of getting from point A to point B, I would catch a ride with Mount Zion Deacon Joe Benn Sr., who lived next door to us. On the Sunday I had promised Lee I would be at church, he had apparently taken me at my word and was in the lobby of the church when Deacon Benn and I arrived. He actually rushed outside, grabbed me by the arm and walked me over and introduced me to Harvey Allen, president of the Men's Usher Board. Lee advised him to immediately put me to work. Allen told me when the next usher board meeting was scheduled and I indicated I was not a member of the church and this was all happening way too fast for me. Further I told Allen I would get back with him should I decide to join Mount Zion.

Lee would not give up. It was now approaching August and Mount Zion's Annual Young People's Day service was coming up. Lee somehow convinced the planning committee to select me as their speaker for this special day. I reluctantly agreed based on the fact that the usher board thing did not work out for him.

This was my first attempt at public speaking. What would be my topic? Their theme as I recall was, "Young People Living for Christ and Looking Forward to a Better Tomorrow." This was a time in our country when young people were rising up and protesting the establishment, whether it was the Vietnam War or racial inequities. The answer came to me while listening to Stevie Wonder's remake of Bob Dylan's song, *Blowin' in the Wind.*

I built my speech around the lyrics of this protest song. I discovered that there were many in the audience who had heard the song; however, they were not that familiar with the lyrics or the theme of Dylan's protest.

After my introduction, I walked up to the microphone. I acknowledged the pastor, officers, and members of Mount Zion. Then I began, "How many roads must a man walk down, before he's called a man?" This lyric immediately resonated with the older deacons who were sitting on the front pews. Many of them were still working in domestic jobs and did not feel they had achieved the respect of society. Their reaction with their verbal expression of "Amen" caught me by surprise. Overall, the speech was well received.

The highlight of this youth day was that the young people of the church had formed a choir under the direction of pianist and arranger, Grady Benn III. Benn played the piano by ear and was very talented. They performed a number of songs. At the end of the program, Rev. Robert E. James, Mount Zion's pastor, provided closing remarks. He was so impressed with the choir that he encouraged them to stay together, committing one Sunday each month for them to perform at a morning worship service. There were thirteen original members who performed at this Youth Day program, and the choir eventually grew to more than fifty young people and recorded a gospel album that I had the honor of producing.

As a part of them formally coming together as a group, it was decided that if they were going to be an official choir in the church, there was a need to establish an organization. The choir sought out Deaconess Katie Haynes, and James Holloway who was a member of the adult gospel chorus, to serve as their sponsors. I became their informal manager. When the group began getting invitations to perform at other churches, I would occasionally drive the church van and later the church bus.

Karen Jones was elected president of the choir. A recent high school graduate, she had enrolled at UT in the fall of 1970. She and I were booked on some local gospel radio programs to discuss the activities of the choir. I would borrow a car from one of my relatives to make these engagements and would pick Karen up at her home. This eventually led to the two of us dating. I was in my sophomore year at UT by this time and there was a five year age difference between us. Her parents were initially hesitant, but they came around since I had a reputation of being a gentleman and a decent guy. Being involved in the church was a plus, since I was now a member and finally serving as an usher.

Karen and I ended up becoming engaged at the beginning of my senior year. Her parents were determined she would get her degree and we assured them our marriage would be based on my receiving my degree and going to work to support the two of us. We got engaged in June 1972 and things were set into motion for a June 30, 1973 wedding. I was scheduled to graduate in May 1973 and was certain that a professional job was waiting for me at the Tennessee Valley Authority.

How did God become our wedding planner? In order to answer this question, I have to take you back to 1966 and a conversation in a warehouse in Phu Vinh, Vietnam. While serving there, a young African-American captain with a specialty in logistics was assigned to our unit. After getting to know him, I found that we had a lot of things in common. First, his full name was Louis James Boston. My full name is James Boston Bussell. He was a graduate of the historically African-American Morgan State University in Baltimore, Maryland. I had a first cousin, Evelyn Berry, who worked in administration at Morgan State. As it turned out, Captain Boston knew my cousin. What a coincidence.

One evening while assisting Captain Boston in conducting a scheduled inventory of the warehouse, he confided in me that his goal upon returning to the States was to become an ordained Baptist minister. His aspiration was to become pastor of the First Baptist Church of Annapolis, Maryland, which served as the church that his family had a long history of attending. I reacted by telling him that should I ever give up my bachelorhood, he could come to Tennessee and perform the ceremony.

I left Vietnam before Captain Boston; however, we committed to stay in touch. Upon leaving Vietnam, Captain Boston became Major Boston and retired as Lt. Colonel Boston. He had a tour in Germany, and we always exchanged Christmas cards with a note giving each other an update on our lives.

Maj. Boston had returned to the United States following his tour in Germany and was assigned to Fort Meade in Maryland. He followed his goal of becoming an ordained Baptist minister and at the time was serving as assistant pastor of the church his family had historically attended. On Christmas Day, 1972 I called and told him that I was now engaged and requested that he come to Knoxville, Tennessee, on June 30, 1973 and preside over our wedding ceremony. We reflected on the discussion in the warehouse in Vietnam and how both our hopes and aspirations were being fulfilled. He immediately accepted my invitation.

God's intervention does not stop there. Prior to asking Boston to preside over our upcoming wedding, a number of events took place at Mount Zion which opened the door for Boston to replace Mount Zion's minister, Rev. R.E. James as the officiant.

Both my family and Karen's parents were long-standing members of Mount Zion. Rev. James had appointed Karen's father to the deacon board and, before he passed, her grandfather was a deacon as well. Naturally, it would be logical that the two families' preference would be to have Rev. James as the officiant at our wedding, possibly leaving Boston with a minor role in the ceremony.

During the period of our dating and engagement, a controversy erupted in the church and members began questioning James's authoritarian leadership style. James made a statement that would come back to haunt him. When a question was raised regarding a decision he had made, he was asked to provide the members attending a meeting an explanation for his decision. His response was: "I don't have to explain anything to anybody in this church." That was the last straw from many of the members. With a major controversy brewing and the criticism being directed towards him, James's reaction was to stand in the pulpit one Sunday morning seeking a vote of confidence from the members. He unexpectedly announced to the congregation that he was retiring, effectively immediately. One of his deacons stood up and made a motion not to accept his offer to retire. The motion never received a second and that vote of confidence never came. His retirement was accepted by the church leadership and the members. He obviously had not prepared himself for this outcome. He immediately accepted an assistant pastor position at a fellow minister's church. During the period immediately following James's retirement, Mount Zion relied on guest ministers to preside over Sunday morning worship services. This opened the door for Boston to be the officiant at our wedding ceremony.

It was also a reunion for the two of us. I had not seen him since my departure from Vietnam in March 1967. He was accompanied by his lovely wife, Belle. Years later, she told me it was the first wedding he had conducted. I am still intrigued by my marriage certificate that reads marriage of Karen Alfreda Jones to James Boston Bussell, Minister, Rev. Louis James Boston. This wedding that God planned is, as of this writing, in its forty-third year. "What God has put together, let no one put asunder."

Boston and I continued our annual communication with him sending our family a Christmas card with an update on his family, and I would make my traditional Christmas Day telephone call to him. He remained either assistant or associate pastor of his family's church in Annapolis until 2006. In January 2006, I received a call from Boston and he told me his pastor, then in his nineties, had retired and he had been called by the membership to replace him. His installation ceremony was scheduled for Sunday, April 2, 2006. I congratulated him and asked that he find a place for me to speak during the ceremony. He was pleased to hear that I would not only be there, but also wanted to participate. Keep in mind that I first met Boston in 1966.

When it was my turn to speak, I was able to stand and say: "God created this day forty years ago in a warehouse in Vietnam." I went on to briefly share our history and the impact he had on our unit in organizing the memorial services for our fallen comrades. Boston continues to be the most dedicated, compassionate, Christian man I have ever meet. He and I have a special bond with respect to our relationship with God.

In 2013 when Karen and I were deciding the best way to celebrate our fortieth wedding anniversary, we chose to go to Annapolis to attend services at Boston's church. Ironically, our June thirtieth anniversary fell on a Sunday that year.

Back in 1973, following our wedding and honeymoon cruise to Nassau, Bahamas, Karen and I settled into our apartment in UT's Married Student Housing Complex's Woodlawn Apartments. Karen had a year of undergraduate studies and a two-year Master's program in psychology ahead of her. In the meantime, it was time for me to go to work. God turned out to be a great wedding planner.

Common Sense is the New Definition of Genius

U pon returning to work, Dow Murphy, the only other personnel officer on the staff, and I had a discussion regarding how my job offer was handled. He told me the Division of Construction wanted to offer me a beginning salary of M-1 Step 4. The Division of Personnel had extended an offer of M-1, but was only willing to go to Step 2. The difference between Step 2 and Step 4 was about $500 annually. The Division of Personnel, being the organization responsible for employment issues, overruled the Division of Construction and required both organizations to offer me the M-1, Step 2. Dow felt that with all of the experience I had with TVA, plus a college degree easily qualified me for the maximum allowable, which was the Step 4. This is when he said our construction management had already discussed promoting me to M-2 at the earliest possible time. At least this was an acknowledgment of me being unfairly treated. With this understanding, it was now time for me to prove myself and justify their confidence.

George Bernard Shaw once said: "You see things; and you say, 'Why?' But I dream things that never were and say, 'Why Not?'"[10] Adopting this philosophy is the only way to survive and be productive in a bureaucracy. One of the things my experience at the Tellico Project and my part-time work taught me was that TVA was a massive bureaucracy. Individuals did their jobs based on standards, which had often been in place since TVA was established in 1933. While working in the cost accounting office, we were responsible for the accounts payable to vendors who were providing multimillion dollar parts for our nuclear power plant construction. In most cases, vendors were expecting payment within thirty days and we were very good at making the thirty-day payment schedule. One of the new cost accounting officers was reviewing invoices assigned to him. He took the initiative to read the vendors' contract and discovered that contractually, the vendor offered a 10 percent discount if payment was received within fifteen days. He had to call this to the attention of the supervisor who did not have a clue that there were similar contractual incentives on most of the contracts. This officer's initiative saved TVA millions of dollars annually. Unfortunately, he never received any recognition for this action. There did not seem to be a lot of interest in saving money. After all, it was not their money. This officer was an inspiration to me and represented the type of employee I wanted to become. I dedicated myself to be a change agent and the lesson learned was not to expect co-workers to embrace new ideas to make things better and more efficient.

In my new job, I was handed the responsibility of recruiting engineers for the Browns Ferry Nuclear Plant in Decatur, Alabama, the Sequoyah Nuclear Plant in Soddy Daisy, Tennessee, and the Watts Bar Nuclear Power Plants in Spring City, Tennessee. The engineering managers were complaining about the lead time in hiring engineers. Visiting with them on site, I immediately discovered the problem. It seems we were only getting one acceptance for every seven offers we extended to college graduates. Our staff in Knoxville would receive engineering applications from central personnel and have a clerk make copies and send them out to the plants. There was no pre-screening. At all three plants that I visited, the engineering managers had weeks and months of applications stacked on the floor in their offices. When they needed an engineer, they would reach into the stack, pull out two or three applications and asked our office to extend an offer to them. By the time the application surfaced it was August, and the candidates had all graduated in May or June and likely had secured jobs three or four months earlier. I immediately went to my supervisor, Tom Addington, and told him I had identified the problem. I suggested we centralize the hiring with prescreening and going as far as inviting candidates to visit the projects. This way the field supervisors would only receive the applications that had been pre-screened and we could extend timely invitations for applicants to visit one or more of the projects. His response was that it would never happen because the supervisors would not relinquish that authority to us. Asked if I could consult with them regarding my idea and he gave me the OK to revisit this with the project engineering managers.

My approach was to walk into the project engineering managers' offices and ask them a simple question. "How would you like for me to get rid of all of those employment resumes lying on the floor of your office?" After that, I explained my strategy of prescreening and inviting engineering applicants, who had an express interest in construction, for a plant visit and interview. The other part of this concept was to sit with them and their lead civil, electrical, and mechanical engineering supervisors to determine their needs for each recruiting cycle and invite candidates for them. Under this new system I would only send the applications of candidates scheduled for a plant visit. They loved it. Addington was shocked that I had pulled it off. The results were that 66 percent of the candidates to whom we offered jobs under this new strategy accepted.

The next recruiting challenge was that our Equal Employment Opportunity Office and the Office of the General Counsel had established what became known as TVA's 1980 goals for representation of women and minorities in the TVA workforce. What a tall task. This was 1973 and only 1 percent of the engineering graduates were minority. The number for women engineering graduates was less than 1 percent.

Now we were competing with well-known companies—IBM, General Motors, General Electric, Rockwell International-and TVA was an unknown entity. In fact, students would ask our campus recruiters: "How many airplanes does TVA have?" (Obviously confusing us with TWA—Trans World Airlines.) This lack of name recognition was a problem even getting students to place us on their list of limited company visits.

The question became, how does one overcomes this hurdle? Jack Hampton, a college recruiter for the Division of Personnel, had just returned from the University of Michigan and had resumes of two African-American engineering applicants. He had made some inroads with these two, who happened to be best friends. Recognizing that I was going to have to be creative in overcoming my competition for these high quality graduates, I felt that if could get them to TVA, I could sell them on our construction organization and the opportunities we had for engineers. I also recognized that it might be a financial hurdle for some students to pay for their airline tickets in advance and then wait for reimbursement during their visit. Now this is when George Bernard Shaw's words rang true. I took the resumes and walked down to the Division of Construction's travel unit. I asked the travel clerk if I could prepay their airline tickets. Her response was no, indicating that TVA could only reimburse for travel. I invited her supervisor into the conversation and he confirmed her opinion, that we could not prepay. When I asked why not, he responded that he would not get it past the auditor in TVA's Division of Finance. I immediately asked where the auditor's office was located. I found his office, paid him a visit, and he confirmed what I had been told by the travel unit. So I asked him to show me the regulation on which he was basing his opinion. He pulled out the travel manual and pointed to a clause that said: "TVA may reimburse any customary travel expenses deemed to be a part of the normal means of conducting business." My next question was: "Where does it say, that we cannot prepay?" He could not find a specific prohibition. I told him that my objective was to enhance our chances of getting minority and women engineers to work for our Division of Construction. He said he could authorize prepayment if he had approval from TVA's general manager indicating that prepaying was a normal means of conducting business if it helped TVA to meet its objectives.

I immediately went back to my office and had my secretary type up a letter from Construction Division Director Horace Mull to TVA General Manager Bill Willis, requesting approval of prepayment of travel expenses. The letter included a recommended approval signature box for Mull. Below Mull's signature, was another box with notation "Approved" above Willis's name and title. Having secured Mull's recommendation, I headed up to the twelfth floor to Willis's office. Upon introducing myself to his secretary, I asked if I could leave the letter with her for Willis's consideration explaining the minority and women recruitment angle as a selling point. She handed the letter back to me and immediately informed Willis over the office intercom that Jim Bussell was in the office and had something that needed his immediate attention. She then told me to go in and get his signature.

Willis did not hesitate to affix signature and reiterated to me how important he thought my efforts were. I excitedly exited Willis's office, had my secretary make copies and took the original up to the auditor in finance and presented him with the approval letter. His response was, you may now prepay any and all travel expenses including airline tickets, motels, and meals. Mission accomplished.

I contacted the two Michigan engineering students asking them to make their airline reservations and submit the details to me, and I would pay for their tickets on our end. They were excited regarding the opportunity.

I then gave Hampton an update and he was impressed that I was able to pull this off. This created a new dilemma for me. Jack had informed the other recruiters on the staff and suddenly they were showing up at my office with applications from other minority and women engineering students. I told them we needed to sit down and develop a strategy to make sense out of this new initiative.

The group tour concept evolved from this meeting. I decided that we would establish a date and invite all the candidates in at the same time. My goal was to prepay the airline tickets and book a block of prepaid hotel rooms for the candidates. The candidates would book their flights to Knoxville with a departure at the end of their classes on Wednesday. The return reservation from Knoxville would be after four o'clock on Friday. The central recruitment staff agreed to take a TVA vehicle and meet the students at the airport to transport them to the hotel. As you might have guessed, many of the students were scheduled to arrive close to midnight. In order to accommodate all of the students and staff, I chartered a forty-six-passenger bus to pick them up at the motel Thursday morning following breakfast, which was charged to their room. They were transported to the TVA Headquarters in downtown Knoxville where the director of the Division of Construction Horace "Buddy" Mull greeted them. I also invited Mull's supervisor, George Kimmons, who was manager of the Office of Engineering Design and Construction. TVA was unique in that we did all design and construction in-house with Kimmons over both the Division of Construction and Division of Engineering Design.

The introductions were followed by an orientation session where the students were provided an overview of current and planned nuclear power plant design and construction projects. Following lunch the students had the opportunity to interview with three separate managers representing our current construction projects. After wrapping up at the office complex around four o'clock, we held a reception for the students at the hotel beginning at seven o'clock. The engineering managers and supervisors were invited to spend some time with them in this informal setting.

On Friday morning, we boarded the bus and traveled to the Watts Bar Nuclear Plant construction site for a project tour, plus question and answer sessions with the personnel there. We returned them back to the Knoxville airport around three o'clock for their return flights to their respective campuses. There were a total of nineteen students involved in this inaugural tour. We offered eighteen jobs, and seventeen accepted, including the two Michigan students. This was mind boggling even for me and I am an eternal optimist. It is amazing how common sense can conquer most challenges. We repeated this process and had about an 80 percent success rate. This was outstanding considering the more visible private sector competition.

One of the areas in which we were deficient was the need for experienced Quality Assurance Engineers. These were engineers representing all of the disciplines, who specialized in reviewing engineering design and construction drawings and specifications to ensure that TVA met the standards of the Nuclear Regulatory Commission (NRC). This was a new concept for TVA. Throughout the agency's history of building dams and fossil fuel plants, there was no oversight from any outside agencies. With the evolving nuclear power plant design and construction, our organization had a difficult time embracing the concept that they now had to be accountable to the NRC.

Gerald Gonsalves, a quality assurance engineer, responded to an ad I had placed in a related engineering publication. He worked as a National Aeronautics and Space Administration contract engineer for the Chrysler Corporation at Cape Canaveral, Florida. Their contract was a part of the NASA Apollo Program and at the time they were preparing for the launch of the American/Soyuz Mission. This launch was scheduled to take place on July 15, 1975, and would connect an American astronaut with a Soviet astronaut once in space. This was also the final launch for the Apollo Program at NASA which resulted in the end of their contract with Chrysler.

Gonsalves was hired, and several weeks later he came to my office to tell me that Chrysler was planning to layoff twenty-eight quality assurance engineers. He indicated that, in an effort to place them with other companies, Chrysler was inviting organizations to the Cape to interview these candidates. I told him that TVA should be represented and I would arrange for him to accompany me. Gonsalves knew the lay of the land and would be a tremendous asset.

He and I made a great team. Since he had worked with all of these engineers, we had a huge advantage. All I had to do was impress the engineers when the companies made their presentations as a part of an assembly in one of the auditoriums on site. The other companies represented were some of the top names in the aerospace indus-try-Rockwell International, Lockheed, Martin-Marietta, and Boeing, to name a few. I was the last to address the group. I opened by stating: "The other companies were here to offer them a job, but I am here, representing the Tennessee Valley Authority, and I was offering them a new career." I went on to tell them that currently, in TVA's seven-state service area, we had seventeen nuclear power construction units either in the design phase or under construction.

Following the meeting, Gonsalves told me all of the available engineers wanted to interview with TVA. I placed a call to Dow Murphy back at my office in Knoxville, and asked if he could be there the next day and bring Jack Hampton from the central employment office to assist with the interviews. Murphy and Hampton arrived the next day as requested. Following the interviews, we extended offers to all twenty-eight engineers and twenty-seven accepted.

While I had many other duties assigned to me, I approached those tasks with the same enthusiasm, trying to identify process improvements to provide a better service to the projects we were supporting. My efforts did not go unnoticed by the project managers and engineering staffs in the field.

I was promoted to M-2 eight months after my initial post-graduation appointment. A year later I was promoted to M-3 and was getting increasingly higher level assignments handed off to me. Murphy was an M-4 and was now our staff supervisor. Tom Addington, who was an M-5 supervisor, had moved over to the labor relations side of the organization. For some reason, they did not feel that Murphy was ready to become an M-5 supervisor. I found myself attending meetings on behalf of the Division of Construction where I was the lowest ranking member there. Most of the other participants were at the M-5 level or higher in these meetings. We were developing strategies and establishing new policies to improve our performance as TVA continued its expansion and need for more personnel in all areas. The agency grew from 26,000 to 52,000 over an eight-year period. Many new hires were trades and labor construction workers–carpenters, electricians, heavy equipment operators, and plumbers.

Recognizing the culmination of my successes, Murphy approached management regarding moving me to the M-4 level. He indicated that he felt it appropriate given that I was making decisions on behalf of the Division of Construction in these meetings which were in the division's best interest. Addington denied his request because he felt I needed "more seasoning."

Murphy informed me of Addington's decision to reject my promotion. Now my leverage in this situation was the common knowledge that George Kimmons, Manager of Engineering Design and Construction, had taken a special interest in me from my days at Tellico Dam. He was the Director of Construction during my tenure there and encouraged his team to find me a part-time employment opportunity while in college. Needless to say, he was impressed that I achieved my degree and that I had rejoined one of his organizations. He considered me his affirmative action success story.

I had a friend, who had received his doctorate degree from the University of Tennessee, working as a vice president of Weirton Steel in Weirton, West Virginia. Dick Symons and I met on a basketball court during our days in married student housing at the university. We became the best of friends and I invited him to join the recreation league basketball team I coached and played on with guys from my old neighborhood. Dick was the only white guy on the team and it was an experience to take him to some of the inner-city neighborhoods where he would be the only diversity in the gym. As a former tight end on his high school football team, and a four-year basketball player at the University of West Virginia, where he received his undergraduate degree, Dick had no problems with his role as a minority and was not intimidated.

I went home with a new strategy to get Addington's attention. I called Dick at his home and told him that I needed a favor. I wanted him to send me a letter on Weirton Steel letterhead inviting me to come up for a visit. He indicated that he had no jobs in my area of expertise. I reiterated to him that I was not asking for job, just a friendly invite to come visit him at Weirton Steel. After I explained my motivation, he agreed to mail the letter to my TVA office the next day.

Knowing that my secretary opens and screens my mail, this letter with Weirton Steel letterhead caught her attention. She brought it over and immediately asked if I was considering leaving TVA and moving to West Virginia. I said I was just looking at some of my options. It did not take long for word to get to Murphy and then on to Addington. The next day, Addington came by my office for a chit-chat. He indicated that Murphy had recommended me for a promotion to M-4 and he had rejected it because he felt I needed more seasoning. My response to him was that this seasoning thing should work both ways. I felt that my seasoning was never a question when he and Murphy assigned me to committees and work groups where everyone on the team were two grades higher than me. I expressed that he and Murphy were both pleased with the way I had represented the division in these forums. Why all of a sudden did seasoning become an issue when a promotion for me is at stake?

Shortly after our meeting, Tom apparently prepared the paper work to promote Murphy to the M-5 level and I received my M-4 promotion. The things an African-American guy has to do to get a promotion, even getting a deserving white guy upgraded in the process.

Taking on the U.S. Veterans Administration

T here is no better understanding of God's faith in me than the hurdles Karen and I had to overcome in order to purchase our home. Ever since we married in 1973, I had looked forward to the day I could utilize one of my major Veterans Administration benefits to purchase a home. When we were married, I had just completed my bachelor's degree from the University of Tennessee and Karen was a UT student majoring in psychology. She recognized from the beginning that to be successful in her field, it would require at least a master's degree. At the time of our marriage, she had a year to go on her bachelor's degree and two years of graduate school in her future.

Taking advantage of her UT enrollment, we lived in a furnished married student housing apartment. When Karen received her master's in May 1976, we were ready to look for a home.

Divine intervention came into play again for me. Gerald Gonsalves and I had become great friends since his arrival at TVA. I was disappointed when construction management decided to transfer him to the newly authorized Hartsville Nuclear Power Plant construction site near Nashville, Tennessee. Gonsalves was the most qualified of all the quality assurance professionals and should have been the manager of the Quality Assurance Branch. The selected manager, in my opinion, was intimidated by Gonsalves's qualifications and did not want him on his immediate staff, resulting in the transfer to the field. Having the last name of "Gonsalves" did not help his case.

On the very day we began our search for a realtor, Gonsalves was in town for a meeting and, as always he came by my office. I told him how excited we were to be looking for a new home. He told me his wife, Bronya, had received her real estate license and was associated with a Knoxville realty firm. He suggested contacting her would be a good place to start. He called Bronya from my office, and I had a chance to speak to her. She was excited because her firm had a nice listing she could not wait to show us. Bronya and I discussed the property and agreed to meet the next evening to look at it.

It turned out to be a custom built house that the contractor had constructed for himself. He had built several homes in the neighborhood. His company was in bankruptcy and because he had used the proceeds from construction loans to build his home, in this same subdivision, the judge had ruled he could not exempt his personal residence from the bankruptcy proceedings.

Karen and I fell in love with this house. The subdivision was on the highest ridge in northeast Knox County, with a great view of the Great Smoky Mountains. We immediately wrote a check for $500 as earnest money to lock in the property.

This is when we encountered a problem. Bronya was not the listing agent. She turned us over to the listing agent who did not seem to be pleased that an African-American couple was going to have access to this prized piece of real estate.

Let the games begin. Karen and I submitted our financials and indicated we were going to apply for 100 percent financing through the VA Home Loan Program. After the financial package was submitted, the realtor sent out an appraiser who came up with an estimate of $10,000 below the current selling price. Prior to our interest, the seller had already reduced the price by some $8,000. It was obvious they knew from my financials that I did not have the $10,000 to complete the 100 percent financing through VA.

Upon receiving my copy of the appraisal, I went over it with a fine-tooth comb. The VA appraisal form consisted of a one-sheet document that required the appraiser to merely check off the appropriate boxes to indicate the features of the property. The appraiser had totally misrepresented the property. His appraisal did not account for 1,000 square feet of unfinished space. He checked a box to indicate that the property had ceiling heat when it actually had central heat and air. Since the VA was now in possession of the appraisal, I called the person at VA assigned to my case. Upon pointing out the discrepancies, he said I needed to go back and convince the original appraiser to submit a revised appraisal to the VA. When I spoke with the original appraiser, he said he stood by his assessment of the property and saw no reason to change.

Fortunately for me, my sister worked in the city of Knoxville property tax office where she was constantly interfacing with property appraisers. I asked her to recommend a person I might hire to do an appraisal for me. I wanted to send the VA an appraisal that would accurately reflect the assessment of the property. It was my hope to convince the VA that they had a poorly performed evaluation from their contract appraiser. She recommended Scott Collins who was highly respected and had achieved the Member Appraisal Institute rating from the Chicago based Appraisal Institute. The MAI was and is the highest rating awarded an appraiser. The VA contract appraiser, I recall, only had a SRA (Senior Residential Appraiser certification).

Collins did a comprehensive appraisal to include a Market Value, Cost Analysis, and Comparison Value based on similar homes sold in the vicinity of the property. I forwarded his appraisal to the VA case worker, who told me that since the VA did not have a contract with Collins, they could not accept his appraisal. I was able, during our discussion, to point out the inaccuracies in the original appraisal the VA had received. He was rather emphatic that my only hope was to get their assigned appraiser to change his assessment.

Next stop: the office of U.S. Congressional Representative John Duncan (R-TN). Duncan had an outstanding track record of helping his constituents deal with problems associated with federal agencies. Upon meeting with his representative in the Knoxville office, she immediately recognized the glaring discrepancies in the VA appraisal. While I was sitting in her office, she picked up the phone and called the Director of VA for this region in Nashville, Tennessee. She told him she was forwarding him the two appraisals and wanted him to explain: "Why Mr. Bussell was having such a difficult time with the Veterans Administration in this matter."

Two days later, I received a phone call at my TVA office from the VA director and he wanted to know what level of appraisal was needed to qualify for 100 percent financing. I gave him the number, and within a week, the finance company had a revised appraisal from VA for my application.

I had chosen not to go to a traditional bank for the VA financing. This was another case of divine intervention. Bill Clemens, a local African-American businessman, had reached out to me at the beginning of my career with TVA. He asked me to speak to the East Knoxville Optimist Club where he was an active member. Clemens's business ventures included investments in real estate. He was apparently impressed with me. When he and I discussed my goal of purchasing a home, he had experience with his friend Bill Curtis. Clements personally introduced me to Curtis, the Caucasian owner of Curtis Mortgage Co.

Now that the appraisal was upgraded, Curtis Mortgage began putting together the financial package to be submitted to VA for approval. Upon completing the package, Curtis realized that Karen and I had another problem. It turned out that after he plugged in the mortgage payment for the home purchase, our debt to income ratio was at 42 percent. He told us that VA had a policy of not approving any application with a debt to income ratio above 40 percent. He stated his firm did not consider our package to be risky. It was his belief we both had great earning potential in our respective careers. He said his company would make the loan if we could get over this new VA hurdle. We completed the process and signed the papers to be submitted to the VA. This was on a Monday, and Curtis informed us that it would take about three weeks before we would get a decision from the VA.

On the following Thursday, three days later, Curtis called to inform me he had an approved application from the VA on his desk. He said they did not even take time to review the package. They must have had an approval stamp waiting when they received it.

Our closing on the house brought about new challenges. We were the first African-Americans to integrate this section of Knoxville. Following the closing, I made my first trip to the house and found a dead black cat in the yard next to the patio. I did not overreact. I knew I would eventually need a shovel, so I hopped back in my car and headed for the nearest hardware store, bought the shovel, brought it home, and buried the cat in the back yard. End of story.

The only other racially inspired incident happened some years later. I initially discussed this one in the introduction of this book. The day after Halloween, I went to the mailbox and discovered that overnight someone had sprayed painted "NIGGER" in large red letters at the edge of my driveway. We lived at the end of a cul-de-sac. Anyone driving through the neighborhood couldn't help but notice. I refused to clean it up.

My decision to ignore and not clean it up was a good one. The neighbors were genuinely upset over the incident, so much so, they conducted their own investigation and determined that the daughter of one of our neighbors, who was attending a private high school, had invited some of her affluent friends over for a gathering. It was their idea of a Halloween prank. The neighbors even discovered the can of red paint in her father's garage. Knowing that they had conducted their own investigation into this incident was quite refreshing. With this new knowledge and information that there were individuals from outside of the community involved, I cleaned the paint off the driveway. Neither one of these incidents required calling the local news media. These were not hate crimes. Just incidents of someone else's stupidity. Neither I nor the news media can fix stupidity.

Other than these two incidents, we have had an excellent relationship with the neighbors. I introduced myself to the fathers in the neighborhood when I noticed some of the teenage boys playing basketball on a goal that was set up in the street. I walked up, acknowledged the fathers and announced, "I've got next." The kids were somewhat taken back to find that this now 30-year-old African-American man came to play. The following weekend, I was downstairs in the den watching a ball game when the front door bell rang. Karen answered and came downstairs to say there was a neighborhood boy with a basketball under his arm wanting to know: "If my husband could come out and play." The answer was a resounding, yes!

Following are a number of what I considered to be God's divine interventions, resulting in the purchase of our home:

- Gerald Gonsalves stopping by my office on the very day we began a quest to buy a home.
- Bronya having her realtor licenses and being affiliated with the listing agency.
- As mentioned earlier, we were living in University of Tennessee married couples housing. Karen had graduated in May. The manager of the UT property told us that as long as we had a contract to purchase a house she could justify the two of us

remaining in her complex. We ended up staying through both the summer and fall quarters. It took almost six months from the time we signed the contract to obtain closure. Our monthly rent there was quite modest for the furnished apartment.

- We were able to set-a-side the projected monthly mortgage payments and pay cash for some of the furnishings due to the six months delay in processing the application.
- Scott Collin's appraisal cost me $150.
- Bill Clemens' introduction to Curtis Mortgage Co. Had we gone to anyone else other than Curtis, I doubt other financial institutions would have gone to bat for us. As an African-American couple, we would have been rejected by the banks without submission to VA.
- Being forced to get Congressman Duncan involved made it possible to get the loan approved without the customary review process which would have possibly caused VA to reject the loan.
- Almost 40 years later, we are still living in the same house which is now mortgage free.

Between a Rock and a Hard Place

O n June 6, 1966, the late U.S. Senator Robert F. Kennedy delivered a Day of Affirmation Address at the University of Capetown, South Africa. I was inspired by several aspects, especially one in particular when he quoted an Italian philosopher: "There is nothing more difficult to take in hand, more perilous to conduct, or more uncertain in its success than to take the lead in the introduction of a new order of things."[11]

My performance in recruiting for TVA's Division of Construction and our success in identifying and hiring minorities and women did not go unnoticed by Bob Betts, the director of the Division of Personnel. Betts had apparently approached George Kimmons regarding transferring me from the Division of Construction to the Division of Personnel. Betts knew that Kimmons and his organization had a lot invested in me and wanted to convince him that the move would allow me to implement some of my successes TVA-wide. Betts was under pressure from the board of directors because they were not seeing much progress in TVA's overall diversity efforts, particularly in the professional career areas.

Dow Murphy approached me and said George Kimmons wanted me to come to his office for a discussion. Arriving at Kimmons' office, I learned of a transfer request from Betts. Kimmons said it would be a good move for both TVA and me. The purpose of the meeting was that Kimmons wanted to assure me that there would always be a place in his organization for me. He also added that he would be looking for future opportunities for me in his Office of Engineering Design and

Construction organization. He closed the meeting by encouraging me take the transfer and give it my best shot.

This meeting was very beneficial. I received the job offer from Betts, and I learned I would be reporting directly to the employment branch chief, Conley Ballinger. It was a promotion to the M-5 level. Betts wanted me to introduce new life into the recruitment process; however, he already had a supervisor of recruitment services in Gerald Shilling. What made this complicated for me was they had structured my position in such a manner that I would not be directly supervising Shilling. We were both at the M-5 level. In order for me to supervise him, they would have to compensate me at a higher level. They had two options to achieve the higher salary for me. They could make me an assistant branch chief or place me on a higher special rate. I would have received a $12,000 annual raise had that been the case. Even with the $8,000 raise I received, Gerald was making more money. I was aware that in a previous situation, two white managers were given the designation of assistant branch chief, and they received the additional compensation. This could have been a deal breaker for me; however, I chose not to press the issue. Ultimately, I felt my performance would eventually result in me getting what I desired. This was a case of choosing to pick my battles. I saw this as another opportunity to prove myself, which to me, was more important and significant than the $4,000 difference in pay. I recently read a quote from Dr. Thomas Sowell, senior fellow at Stanford University's Hoover Institute, which can be applied to how I have approached my work experience and dealt with this unfair treatment. Sowell states: "If you want to spend your life nursing grievances, you will never run out of grievances to nurse, regardless of what color you skin is."[12]

I was impressed with the great lengths they went through to pull this off. My introduction into this new assignment was certainly disruptive to the status quo. In hindsight, the logical thing to do in this case was to bring me over as a replacement for Shilling and make me the supervisor of recruitment services. Had that been the case, the pay differential would have never been an issue.

I began by having meetings with Shilling and his staff of recruiters. Many were excited regarding my addition to the staff, as they had partnered with me on the recruiting successes we achieved in the Division of Construction. The staff was very open to some of the ideas and strategies I had discussed during these meetings. I would later learn that, following the meetings, Shilling advised them not to get excited about the ideas I had expressed and told them I was still "wet behind the ears." Upon hearing this feedback, I encouraged the staff to be patient with me and that there would be a way to get around this situation.

It all came to a head after being there a couple of months. I took a day of vacation and returned to learn that, while I was away Shilling was given a performance evaluation without any input from me. Shilling took the opportunity to go back to his office, wave the evaluation, and announce that I had no input. His message was that they were not to take me seriously.

Now it was my time to make a move. I sought out a person in the division that I could use as a conduit to convey my frustrations with Betts. I informed the individual that I was considering returning to my old job in the Division of Construction and I did not feel that it was appropriate to go over my supervisor's head to approach Betts regarding my concerns. I further stated that should Betts call me to his office for an update, I would be happy to oblige him. Two hours later, I was summoned to Betts's office for a status report.

Betts and I had a full and frank discussion. I told him that the way things were structured, I was between a rock and a hard place and did not see any light at the end of the tunnel. He asked me for a suggestion to get things on track. The answer is a simple one: Get rid of Shilling and make me the supervisor of recruitment.

Two weeks later, Ballinger came into my office and said Shilling was being transferred to a personnel officer position in another organization and wanted my thoughts on how to fill the void in recruitment services. I indicated that the best move would be to not fill Shilling's position at this time. That I would physically move in with the staff and serve as Supervisor of Recruitment Services for the time being. He said he would tell Betts of our new direction. Wonder where Bob had heard this before?

I learned a great lesson about leverage from an unusual source. Traveling a lot, a passenger shared an experience he had on one of his business trips. He was flying out of Los Angeles and there was a line at the skycap station. One of the other passengers became very unruly and abusive to the African-American skycap. Everyone in line felt for this older gentleman who apparently chose to ignore that unruly passenger, while diligently processing the man's bags and eventually handing him his boarding pass. One of the passengers, who was a couple of persons back in line, walked up to the skycap and tried to apologize for the behavior of the unruly passenger. He expressed how much he admired how the skycap had managed the situation by remaining calm and respectful throughout the ordeal. The skycap then spoke up and said everything was alright. He had been with the airline for over thirty years and always tried to do a good job. Then he said the rude passenger would remember him when he gets to New York, because his bags are on their way to San Francisco. This was not the last time I would have to apply leverage during this assignment.

I reviewed the mission of our recruitment organization. There were four major functions for the recruitment office. There was college recruiting where we were visiting sixty-four colleges and universities annually and some we visited twice. We ran a co-op education program for engineering, business, and science majors. We managed a college and high school student summer intern program. Finally, we were responsible for experienced recruiting. I identified four senior staff members to be the lead in each of these areas with the goal of drawing on the resources of overall office personnel to support their efforts. Another area was added when we established the group tour concept which had been so successful for me at the Division of Construction. I had some selling to do before we could implement this program TVA-wide.

First, I met with Betts and informed him that if we were going to be successful, the Division of Personnel was going to have to centralize certain functions and take away some of the flexibility the seventeen individual divisions had in their recruitment process. I needed his backing in order to limit the distribution of minority and women applicants exclusively to the divisions that signed up for the group tour concept. I did not want to send these applications out and have individual divisions randomly inviting these students to visit TVA when we had a process in place to give all the divisions exposure to the applicants. Basically, should a division choose not to participate, they would not have a chance to review the minority and women applications.

Secondly, I purchased a copy of the Sunday edition of the *Atlanta Journal-Constitution* where I found fifteen advertisements from different TVA divisions seeking applicants for engineering positions. The cost of these ads ran into thousands of dollars for TVA. After making a few courteous telephone calls to a sample of the divisions who had run the ads, I inquired about their results. Their response was that they could not answer the question. I knew this was the case because the ads were not coded with any identifying reference, which would indicate that the resume was a direct result of a response to a specific ad. My goal was to centralize all recruiting advertising under our recruitment branch. It would essentially be a new service that we would offer the divisions in order to allow them to get more bang for the buck. Specifically, we would not go to a business center like Atlanta to recruit experienced engineers; instead, we would target advertise in specific areas where nuclear power related industries existed.

Betts agreed that this needed to happen and informed me he was going to schedule a TVA-wide personnel officers meeting and allow me to break the news to all of the divisions in one room. This would allow for an exchange of dialogue between affected personnel officers and myself.

Some initial reaction was negative. That was to be expected, given that we were taking away some of their autonomy. However, as the meeting progressed many were persuaded that this was an improvement. I suspected that some of the resistance came from the fact that this African-American guy is now seemingly dictating to the "good ole boy" network.

Some of the strongest resistance came from a personnel manager for the Division of Engineering Design, the sister organization to the Division of Construction under George Kimmons's leadership. This personnel manager indicated he had his own process and would not be participating in the group tours. I said fine; however, he would not be receiving applications from our women and minority candidates because they will be locked in exclusively to the group tour concept. He replied that I could not do that. I closed the conversation by telling him I respected his decision. However, it would be up to him to explain to his division director why they were not recruiting women and minority candidates. Needless to say, he finally came around and participated in the first tour.

Arriving back to the office following the personnel officer conference, I told the staff we had our mandate and it was full steam ahead.

We immediately established a series of dates for the group tours averaging about one every two weeks. Since there was a large need for engineers at the Office of Power which was based in Chattanooga, Tennessee, we decided to rotate the tours between Knoxville and Chattanooga.

One advantage of establishing the tour dates in advance of our college recruitment schedule was that the recruiters had a special brochure with all of the relevant information that could be handed out to specific candidates who qualified for participation.

The staff was highly motivated and excited to be a part of something so progressive. However, I encountered something that no manager should have to deal with from a subordinate. Ron Brock, one of two professional white males on staff and the lead person for our experienced recruiting, had accepted another job within TVA was leaving the staff. Malcolm Branner, an African-American lead over the Co-operative Education Program, immediately approached me regarding making a move to become the lead experienced professional recruiting coordinator. I thought this was a reasonable request, as it would be just as easy to fill Malcolm's position. I called a meeting of the staff to announce some changes informing them that Branner would be replacing Brock. In addition, due to the large volume of phone calls from students making their reservations to participate in the group tours, the two least senior clerks would be moved back to the receptionist area to help with timely responses to the students.

One of the clerks was African-American and was upset that she would be moved back to the receptionist area, since that was where she started with the organization and she thought that she had paid her dues. The other clerk was a white female whose husband made a call to Betts indicating that as an African-American, I was discriminating against the Caucasians on staff. The African-American clerk personally met with Betts to complain that I was discriminating against the African-Americans. Betts summoned me to his office to share the feedback he had received regarding this decisions with the clerks. I believe to this day, that I may be the only person on the face of this earth accused of discrimination by both a Caucasian and an African-American over the same decision. This is why I moved both clerks back to the receptionist area when I could have probably gotten by with one. I anticipated the potential of a real problem that would have made matters complicated had I chosen the Caucasian clerk over the African-American clerk and vise-versa.

A couple of days after the meeting announcing the changes, Tom Clark, an African-American professional staff member, knocked on my door and asked if I had a second. I said yes, come on in and take a seat. I was not prepared for what came next. The first thing that he said to me was: "I have lost confidence in you as a supervisor." Then he asked me if Branner was running the office or if I was in charge. Branner just happened to be on travel status this particular day. He questioned my decision to give Branner the experienced recruiting position without assessing the interest of others professionals on the staff. When he finished what he had to say, he asked me for my response. I calmly looked across my desk and said to him: "Tom, you have 30 days to find a new job." Then I politely asked him to leave my office.

Apparently his clerk and some of the people outside of the office who did not have a favorable opinion of me, had gotten Tom pumped up to have this confrontation. I understand that prior to coming into my office he had boasted to the staff about what he planned to say.

This meeting took place about 10 a.m. Before I went to lunch, a staff member came in to say how proud she was of me. No one knew how I would react to such a challenge to my authority, particularly by another African-American professional and personal friend. She indicated that Tom was caught off guard regarding my response.

The day did not end there. Around two o'clock, I was again approached by Tom and asked if we could have another conversation. I said yes, come on in. He began the discussion by saying: "We kind of let things get out of hand this morning and might have said some things we really didn't mean." I interrupted him and responded that he might have said some things he would like to take back; however, from my standpoint, the damage had already been done. First of all, I was insulted, being an African-American manager, for an African-American subordinate and friend to tell me that he did not have confidence in me as supervisor. I went on to say that his previous statement was something he would never say to one of his white managers, even though he might be thinking it. Secondly, as a manager, I did not want someone working for me who didn't have confidence in my leadership. Then I asked him why he would want to work for someone in whom he did not have confidence. Thirdly, I felt that we had developed a great team and were doing some very positive things for TVA. The meeting ended with me saying: "You have let me know that you are not a team player and there is no longer a place for you here. Tom, you have 30 days."

Without his knowledge, I explained the situation to Betts and asked if he could find another place for Tom somewhere in the agency. He was transferred to a personnel officer position in another division. What continued to amaze me as I encountered these obstacles, was that I never let myself get angry, which I attributed to God's guidance. By not getting angry, I was able to focus on strategies to address obstacles that came my way.

Our staff continued to have phenomenal success in all aspects of our recruiting efforts. We had an 85 percent success rate with our group tour recruiting concept. The caliber of our graduates was even more impressive to our managers, who were seeing some engineering students with 4.0 grade point averages.

A white female student who participated in one of our first tours pulled me off to the side at the conclusion of her visit. She indicated it was a great experience and she had a fiancée who was an engineering major with a 4.0 GPA, and he could also benefit from the group tour experience. I accepted her constructive criticism and we opened the tour concept up to all students who met our criteria, including white males.

The summer months proved to be relatively quiet with the exception of the summer intern programs. Most of the work on them was completed by the middle of June, when the interns were all in place. This lull provided the staff an opportunity to pursue another venture that I deemed unique and would enhance our presence on the campuses we visited.

During this lull, I got with the lead recruiter for the group tour concept and we set up a process to invite a select group of college campus placement office directors in for a visit. We would let them experience the process that we used for the student group tours, prepay their airline tickets, book a block of prepaid rooms, and have them experience the same overviews of our various TVA organizations as the students had received. They also had the opportunity to tour the Sequoyah Nuclear Plant Construction site.

With our focus on engineering students, we selected forty directors from the major engineering schools. This proved to be an overwhelming success. For the first time, these officials gained an understanding of the substantial scope of our engineering employment opportunities. They were able to see the diversity of the engineering jobs at TVA. The impact of their visit was fully appreciated when the fall recruiting schedules were posted on campus. On a number of occasions, the campus placement office informed us that our schedule was overflowing and that we either needed to send an extra recruiter or extend our campus visit by a day or two.

Earlier, I mentioned that we were going to take the lead in assisting the various divisions in meeting their experienced engineering recruiting needs. Since most of our energies were focused on engineering related to nuclear power plant design, construction and operation, our needs included all disciplines of engineering. Through our research, we discovered that the experienced engineers we were seeking were working for companies such as Stone and Webster, Brown and Root, Bechtel, Westinghouse, and General Electric with locations including Houston, Texas; Newport News, Virginia; and Boston, Massachusetts.

Our concept was a very efficient one for the potential applicants, as well as our engineering managers who would travel with us to the interview site. Like the group tour concept, we would establish dates for these recruitment trips in advance. Our staff would identify target locations and invite the various participating divisions to submit their needs by engineering disciplines. We would run a full page ad in the Sunday morning edition of the locally targeted city's newspaper. One of the advantages of centralizing advertising, was that we could provide TVA with greater exposure for essentially the same money the divisions were spending on their individual ads.

The key that made this process efficient was that we would identify a hotel in the city with a convenient location. We would work with the hotel to provide us with a dedicated telephone line and number, which would be included in the newspaper ad for applicants to call us locally. We would have an advance team of two recruiters there on Sunday morning available to man the telephone line. They would establish appointments for the potential applicants beginning at 6:00 p.m. the following Tuesday.

TVA managers were standing by with airline reservations scheduled to arrive early Tuesday afternoon. By late Monday evening, we would have a good idea of the level of response. If a manager did not get a good response for his or her needs, they simply canceled their reservation. In a number of cases, if they only had one or two responses, we would set up a schedule for the candidate to come to TVA. This was a win-win for everyone.

When the managers arrived, they found highly qualified engineers with experience directly related in the areas of TVA's needs. The candidates were impressed that a federal agency could be so organized and able to make the process so convenient for their schedule. Having the ads in the Sunday paper for them to call, establishing the interviews after 6:00 p.m. and being available for them up to 10:00 p.m., when the last one was scheduled, were all good selling points.

One weekend, we had two teams working two locations. One group was in Newport News, Virginia, and the other in Houston, Texas. It is hard to explain how proud I was of the efforts of the staff. Our success was very contagious and we were a well-oiled machine.

It is amazing how common sense can make you look like a genius.

New Adventure, New Challenges

J ust when I thought the Division of Personnel could find no other way to discriminate against me, I was proven wrong. Bob Betts called me down to his office to tell me he wanted me to consider taking on a special assignment being directed by the three member board of directors. The board had earlier appointed a Blue Ribbon Citizens Commission in Chattanooga, Tennessee, to investigate claims of systemic discrimination against African-Americans there. The Commission had completed its review and found these claims to be substantiated. They also submitted twenty-eight recommendations to address the issues facing TVA's African-American employees in Chattanooga. Finally, they recommended that a project manager be appointed to oversee the implementation of those recommendations. The board of directors agreed and asked Betts, as director of the Division of Personnel, and George White, director of TVA's Equal Employment Opportunity Office, to make a recommendation for the project manager position. Apparently, I was their choice. Betts felt that, due to the visibility, the assignment had some risk. I saw it as another challenge and told Betts that he had supported me since my arrival, and I had confidence he would have my back in this endeavor, as well.

With all the parties in agreement, TVA issued a press release announcing my assignment as the project manager for the commission's recommendations. In the meantime, Betts had agreed to my recommendation that Malcolm Branner become acting supervisor of Recruitment Services while I worked full time on this new project. Branner was an M-3 and this would mean a temporary promotion to the M-5 level. I was excited for Branner who, like me, was an

African-American Vietnam veteran who had returned to the University of Tennessee and received his bachelor's degree following his discharge. He had initially worked for Bell South before being recruited to TVA. This was going to be an eighteen month to two year assignment for me. Frankly, I did not see myself returning afterward.

A couple of weeks later, TVA decided to terminate Betts' employment. His departure from TVA threw a wrinkle into things for me. My supervisor, Conley Ballinger was promoted to acting Director of Personnel. This is when I learned that they were taking a second look at the recruitment supervisor position. The organization, within the Division of Personnel, responsible for reviewing the classification of management positions indicated that Branner would be promoted to M-4 instead of M-5 in his temporary assignment. Ironically, they had no problem with Caucasian Gerald Shilling, being an M-5 when he held the same position.

Keep in mind, since Shilling's departure, the scope of responsibility of the staff had been expanded under my leadership including the group tour concept, taking over corporate recruitment advertising, and centralizing experienced recruitment. Branner and I went to dinner where I broke the news to him. I told him I would pursue the M-5 promotion further, and he said I would be fighting a losing battle. I had never let losing battles stop me before.

When I got home that evening I got out my trusty typewriter and wrote a letter to General Manager Bill Willis, saying it would probably be in the TVA's best interest to replace me as manager on the Commission's Project. The letter went on to say that since Betts was no longer Director of Personnel, I was personally encountering some of the same issues in Knoxville that the Board wanted me to address in Chattanooga. The first thing the next morning, I sought and received an appointment with Willis for two o'clock that afternoon.

Having secured the appointment, I walked down to Ballinger's office to express my dissatisfaction with the turn of events regarding Branner's appointment. I shared with him that it fit a pattern of discrimination towards me throughout my history with the Division of Personnel. I showed him the letter I had written to Willis and told him I had an appointment with the general manager at two o'clock that afternoon. I said he was welcome to join me at that meeting since he had a stake in what would ultimately transpire. After reading the letter, he told me I could not resign; that TVA had made a public announcement and it would be embarrassing for me to step-down. I said what would be embarrassing is the reason I chose to step down. I mentioned specifically the treatment I received by not being properly compensated when I joined his staff and now the games the division was playing with Branner's temporary promotion.

What Ballinger didn't know was that I had no intention of giving that letter to Willis. In the light of Betts's firing, I was really seeking a vote of confidence from a higher authority than the director of personnel.

While the letter did not specifically say I was resigning, the wording was: "I thought that it would be in TVA's best interest to replace me." With that as my lead in to Willis, I expressed concern that the African-Americans in Chattanooga knew that one of the principals responsible for me getting the assignment was no longer with TVA, and I questioned whether or not my credibility had been destroyed. Willis gave me the response I was looking for when he said that he and the board of directors were taking this matter in Chattanooga seriously and if I encountered any difficulties, I had direct access to his office. With that understanding, I agreed to move forward.

Ballinger was now obviously relieved that I did not pull the letter from my suit jacket pocket. As the elevator doors closed outside of Willis's office, Ballinger turned and asked when I wanted Branner's promotion to M-5 effective. I told him: "This is Wednesday, so make it effective retroactive to Sunday, since that was the beginning of that bi-weekly pay period." Mission accomplished.

Now on to the task at hand. There were a wide range of recommendations handed down by the Commission. Most of them required staff support and coordination for things like sensitivity training and management rating systems. My goal as project manager was to work with the individuals selected to coordinate these activities to ensure that they had access to all of the resources they needed. My focus was to basically identify specific issues and concerns the African-American employees had in Chattanooga. I felt that it was a plus for them to have an African-American project manager to be a conduit for working to get these individual issues resolved. I recognized that the Commission had to deal with generalities and not with specific individual cases. I wanted to meet with the African-American TVA employees to identify the actual discriminating supervisors and managers. All the white managers in Chattanooga should not be tarnished by the actions of a few.

One of my first actions was to establish group meetings with middle and upper managers representing the various divisions in the Chattanooga area. I told them my strategy would be to bring in a team of TVA Equal Employment Opportunity counselors to Chattanooga and open up opportunities for the African-Americans to come forward and identify, who and how they were discriminated against by specific managers. This was the only way, in my opinion, that TVA could move forward and not have to revisit this issue in the not too distant future.

I then met with the local African-American organizations including the TVA Black Employees Association, the TVA Black Managers Association and any non-affiliated employees who wanted to attend. At these meetings, they were told that office space had been secured in Chattanooga for a team of EEO counselors to meet with employees during normal work hours, or after work should they prefer, to take information regarding their individual cases and I gave them the dates when the counselors would be available. During the meetings, some employees made it clear that they were afraid of being blacklisted by TVA and not being promoted should they come forward. My question to those individuals was quite simple: "Was it better to be blacklisted and not get promoted or not be blacklisted and not get promoted? Where was the difference?" The bottom-line was that I was not there to fight their battles for them. Without the names of the discriminating officials, TVA would be at a loss in terms of getting the results they were looking to receive through this process.

An employee who worked in the central mail room for TVA's offices told me that African-Americans made up about ninety percent of the workers there and they performed in very hazardous conditions. He invited me to visit their work site, which I did the next day.

This employee gave me a tour of the mail room and pointed out how congested the area was when all of the mail was picked up in the afternoon from the various Chattanooga offices. He noted that the congestion created a fire hazard because of the difficulty in evacuating the building. He pointed out that the width of the mail carts, which were barely able to fit through the doorway of the mailroom, meant that occasionally fingers were smashed. He then took me outside and pointed out that the lifts on the trucks were on the rear driver side which placed the mail clerks in traffic at the end of the day during mail pick-up time.

The following week, I returned to Chattanooga with Dan Barker, a manager in TVA's Facilities Management Division. Once all of these mailroom matters were pointed out to him, he immediately recognized the problems. Within three weeks, carpenters had come in and widened the door ways, and partitions were knocked down to expand the work space inside the mailroom. Finally, the mail trucks were modified to place the lifts on the opposite side to get the workers away from rush hour traffic. I became a hero to the mailroom workers. It was a classic example of how specific issues can be resolved.

Unfortunately, when the EEO team came to Chattanooga, no African-Americans showed up to meet with them; however, specific formal complaints of discrimination from two Caucasian females were processed. This was disappointing, as it let a number of potentially guilty managers off the hook. It also gave the TVA general manager and board of directors an out, as they could claim they had done their part by committing the necessary resources to resolve these complaints.

For the balance of the time I spent on this project, I monitored the activities of the lead persons implementing the other action items. These items were well into the implementation stage and nearing completion when I received a call from Doug Horne, Chief of the Management Planning Staff for the Office of Engineering Design and Construction. George Kimmons, as promised, wanted me back in his organization and had found an opportunity as an Administrative Analyst on Doug's staff. It was also a promotion from M-5 to M-6. As staff chief, Horne was an M-7. This action was effective on July 29, 1979.

Four months later, Doug accepted a position on the general manager's staff, and I was promoted to Chief, Management Planning Staff on November 18, 1979, at the M-7 level. God had found a way to reward my efforts, despite my distractors who were determined to derail my plans for a productive career.

I received some exciting news in July 1980. Kimmons had an executive opening on his immediate staff and was recommending me to the general manager and board of directors for an entry level executive management position to become one of his assistants. TVA had a policy that all candidates for executive management had to be interviewed by the three-member Board of Directors. At that time the TVA Board of Directors were presidential appointments, who are confirmed by the U.S. Senate to serve seven year full time terms. (Today there are nine part-time directors who each serve five year terms.)

Following my interview with the Board, Kimmons came to my office to tell me that he had received feedback directly from one of the board members. He told me that this member asked him where he had been hiding me all of this time. I had gotten the seal of approval and the paperwork was being processed to promote me to the M-8 level effective July 20, 1980. Ironically, the organization that had originally rejected the temporary promotion of Branner to the M-5 level now had the honor of processing all three of these promotions. I was confident that down the road, there would later be a price to pay from the Division of Personnel.

The question being raised: Was I being brought along too fast? The answer lies in fact that TVA was going through a tremendous expansion. I had mentioned earlier that we went from 26,000 employees to more than 52,000 during this period. There were certainly more challenges, and with the expansion came opportunities for managing the resources needed to maintain efficiency. I feel that I had proven my ability to adapt in a changing environment. In fact, I was one of a few managers who embraced change. In other words, I was not the only one advancing as a result of this expansion. Doug Horne's advancement opportunities were another example.

As an assistant to the Manager of Engineering Design and Construction, I had two staffs reporting to me. One was the Engineering Reports and Technical Information Staff and the other was the Management Planning Staff. One of my first goals was to review these two staffs to determine if the functions could better be implemented under one M-7 manager rather than two. The consolidation was implemented when the engineering reports manager accepted another position in TVA.

I was now Kimmons' representative on the TVA-wide salary policy Labor Relations Committee, which was responsible for the annual contract negotiations with the unions that represented the salaried employees. I also served as his representative on the Joint Management/Labor Health Insurance Committee, which was responsible for working with Blue Cross/Blue Shield in managing TVA's $28-million self-insured employee health insurance plan. Blue Cross/Blue Shield served as plan administrator.

While on Kimmons's staff, I continued to develop my leadership skills. I was elected president of the Knoxville TVA Chapter of the National Management Association. I was also active with the TVA Employees Credit Union. I began there as a volunteer on the credit committee, and I was eventually elected by the membership to serve a three-year term on their board of directors. In my final year on the Board, I was elected by fellow board members to serve as their chairman. At that time, the TVA Employees Credit Union had assets totaling almost $100 million dollars.

In addition, Bill Willis and Kimmons had asked me to serve as management co-chairperson of the Knoxville TVA Combined Federal Campaign. The CFC is the annual fundraising effort of federal agencies for charitable contributions for local and national not-for-profit organizations. The TVA campaign had raised $520,000 the previous year. This campaign year came on the heels of highly emotional labor negotiation sessions with the salaried employee unions. The negotiations were so hotly contested that TVA negotiators had to resort to threating to exercise the right to cancel the labor agreement entirely. This was not the best time to go ask the employees for money. Wonder why I was chosen to be that year's campaign management co-chairman? My union representative co-chairperson was Garnett Morgan. We were both on our respective negotiating teams during these labor talks and sat across the table from one-another. The great thing about working with Morgan was that we did not take what had happened during the negotiations personally. She and I both felt that the task of raising these funds was for the greater good.

One of the hurdles associated with the low employee morale, many believed that not giving would be a reflection of their disappointment with TVA management. Despite these challenges, Morgan and I were still able to raise a little over $500,000, short of the $525,000 goal we had set for the campaign that year. Overall, we were pleased with the results, with the local United Way organization being extremely pleased. The United Way was a major benefactor; however, their share of funding was not significantly affected considering the amount we had raised. Kimmons had criticized me for setting the goal that high.

He thought that there was a long standing practice of not missing the goal. My response was the goal was only five thousand dollars more than what had been raised the previous year. To set a goal lower than the previous year was acknowledging defeat before the campaign got underway. I informed him that acknowledging defeat was not the way I approached anything I am striving to achieve. My challenge to myself is always to seek ways to overcome the obstacles that lie ahead.

It became obvious to me that this last promotion was the end of the line for me at TVA. Kimmons had previously been very supportive throughout my career. He gained from our relationship as well. Whenever the diversity issue was raised with senior management by the general management and the Board, Kimmons always used me as his ace in the hole. He would boast about how he had this African-American guy in his organization who was a mover and shaker and was being advanced through his organization as opportunities presented itself. The other senior managers could not compete with Kimmons in this regard; they did not have a James Bussell. When I reached the M-8 level, Kimmons was wise enough to know that no organization in TVA would try to recruitment me away. He knew that none of his contemporaries would be willing to pay an African-American male at the M-8 level or higher. M-8 was Kimmons' and TVA's glass ceiling for me.

Rejection Is Merely an Opportunity for New Direction

In early 1984, General Manager Bill Willis and the TVA Board of Directors announced a major reorganization of TVA's two major offices. The Office of Engineering Design and Construction would be consolidated under the Office of Power. Hearing that his organization would no longer operate with autonomy under his current leadership, George Kimmons decided to retire. I was about to learn what the late African-American poet Maya Angelou meant when she said: "Rejection can simply mean new direction."[13]

As a part of this reorganization, Willis and the Board further announced that the functions of the Division of Personnel, Office of Equal Employment Opportunity, and the Division of Labor Relations would be consolidated into one organization at the M-12 level. Seeing this new structure, I forwarded both Willis and the Board a letter of application to become manager of this newly created office. I spelled out what I thought qualified me for consideration. TVA had historically used the excuse that there were not many opportunities for women and minorities for senior level positions, due to the technical nature of the business model. Most senior level positions were filled by engineers, including Willis.

I emphasized my experience in all three areas covered by the newly created organization. I reminded them of my project management experience for the Blue Ribbon Commission's efforts in Chattanooga, my experience in the Division of Personnel—which was well documented-and finally, serving on both the Salary Policy Labor Relations negotiating team and the Joint Labor/ Management Health Insurance Committee. I discussed my leadership skills as demonstrated by being president of the Knoxville Chapter of the National Management Association and my tenure as Chairman of the Board of Directors for the TVA Employees Credit Union.

Did I get a response to my letter of application from the general manager or the board of directors? If this was a multiple choice question, the correct answer would be, "none of the above."

They later placed a white male engineer in this senior management position, ignoring a number of qualified minorities and women. Ironically, prior to the selection for the position, I was informed in an unrelated interview with Willis, that I was being offered a demotion to eventually report to the yet to be named manager.

The interview with Willis was a result of a unique series of circumstances that would lead me to my ultimate departure from TVA. Since the Office of Engineering Design and Construction would be under the leadership of the Chattanooga-based Office of Power, the Division of Personnel saw this as an opportunity to get back at me for the frustration I had caused them over the Shilling transfer and the Branner promotion.

Marilyn Taylor, an African-American female, was named the permanent Director of Personnel to succeed Betts. She was recruited from outside of the agency, although there were several women and minority candidates inside of TVA who were more qualified for this director position. This became particularly true when word circulated rather quickly from informed circles inside the Division of Personnel that Taylor did not have a degree.

Following the announcement of the reorganization, there was a strategy meeting for personnel officers at a resort near Sweetwater, Tennessee. During the meeting, Taylor approached me and requested I join her for breakfast the next morning at a restaurant that was away from the location where the conference was being held.

We met as scheduled. The purpose of the meeting was for Taylor to assure me I was going to be OK within the reorganization. She said she had my back and would get with me as soon as all of the details regarding my position were finalized. I thanked her and we returned to the strategy meeting. Keep in mind that I had been a thorn in the side of most of her senior managers. My take on the meeting: Taylor having my back was not a good sign for me. This discussion took place in early March 1984.

The next time she and I spoke regarding my future was at Board Chairman Dave Freeman's retirement reception in mid-May. His seven year term on the TVA Board of Directors had expired and he was not recommended by President Ronald Reagan to serve a second term. This is when it got interesting for me. Taylor approached and informed me that she had some good news and bad news. The good news was that they had identified three possible positions for me. The bad news was that all three would be at the M-7 level, resulting in a one grade demotion. I asked her what the three positions were. She indicated the details had not be fully defined. It was obvious she was not a human resources specialist. In order to classify a position for deter-mining the grade level, you first have to define the scope of work and establish the responsibilities of the position. Not having done that, I thought to myself, their sole goal was to demote me. She said she had been in discussions with General Manager Willis regarding my situa-tion, and that I should expect a call from him. My response to her was very calculated. I said that would be fine. Her interpretation was that I was accepting of the direction my career was taking at the M-7 level.

The next encounter with Taylor was a casual meeting at the TVA Employees Credit Union during the lunch hour in June. We were both in line when she turned and asked if I had heard from Willis. I told her, no. She said she would get back with Willis to ensure he followed-up with me. Later that afternoon, I received a call from Willis's office asking me to come over and meet with him. We established a date and time which was a couple days away.

Willis began the meeting by telling me there was some thinking in the agency that I had been brought up too fast in the organization and that I needed "more seasoning" (seems like I had that term applied to me before) to prepare me for the executive management level. My superior and outstanding performance evaluations at the execu-tive level told a different story. Of course, I knew the source of such thinking. Willis said I would be working under his wings for a couple of years and we could discuss moving back into executive management at that time. He wanted an opportunity to get to know me.

He further stated that the job they were considering for me would initially require me to report to Hugh Parrish, who was the manager of the Office of Power in Chattanooga and was Kimmons' counterpart before the reorganization. Willis then asked me what my goals were for the future. This is when I reminded him that I had sent both him and the Board of Directors a letter of application for the newly formed position of Manager of Personnel, Labor Relations and Equal Employment Opportunity. The shocker for me was in his response. This is when I learned that I would eventually report to the yet to be named manager of that organization. Willis wanted me to assist the new manager in improving the employee morale, which was negatively impacted by this massive reorganization. Now I was thinking, who is going to work on my morale?

I had difficulty believing what I was hearing. This is the same Bill Willis, who was an Assistant Director of the Division of Construction, should have been fully aware of my contributions at Tellico Dam and the part-time assignment in the Construction Accounting Branch during college. He was the same Bill Willis, who as General Manager, authorized the prepayment of travel for me to recruit minorities and women. The same Bill Willis who approved me to be the project manager of the Chattanooga Blue Ribbon Commission's report and to oversee the implementation of their twenty-eight recommendations. Bill Willis also asked Kimmons to loan me out to co-chair the Knoxville TVA Combined Federal Campaign. This is the same Bill Willis who, as Chairman of the WATTec Conference, asked me to serve on the WATTec Executive Committee.

WATTec was a local annual conference covering areas of interest for the various engineering, science and technical organizations in the community. Ironically, the executive committee was made up of corporate presidents and CEO's of local technical and scientific companies, as well as federal agency executives, like himself. Willis was aware of my interest in helping high school students identify career options to pursue after their high school experience. (It was a perfect fit for me. At the time I was also producing and hosting a local television public affairs program focusing on career options for the 80's and beyond.) The WATTec Conference had a goal to expose these students to careers in the various engineering and scientific areas represented by the conference. Willis wanted me to head up the annual committee to involve high school students in this technical conference. Through the television program, I had established a relationship with most of the area high school guidance counselors.

At the end of the conference, I received a letter from Willis stating: "What an outstanding job you did this year in putting new life into our WATTec student/education activities. The High School Math and Science Workshops were excellent and the credit for this success is yours." Now all of a sudden, I am not ready for a position at the executive level where I had been serving for four years. Willis closed the meeting by telling me that he would get with Taylor, and they would send me an offer letter for the position. At this point, they still did not have a job description for me.

Two days later, I received a letter from Willis offering me the job. Taylor had played right into my hands. Upon reading the letter from Willis, I gave Taylor a call and told her that before I could give Willis a response to his offer, I needed the Division of Personnel to issue me a Notice of Reduction-in-Force letter. She indicated that there were no plans to issue a RIF since I had a job offer from TVA. I informed her that should I accept the demotion being offered by Willis, I wanted something in my personnel folder indicating the circumstances under which I accepted the lower grade position. She said she would have the RIF issued.

Later that afternoon, Taylor arranged for my RIF to be delivered. I was now ready to respond to Willis. I wrote, informing him that I was declining his job offer. I had decided to take the reduction-in-force. In the letter I expressed my concern that he and TVA were essentially asking me to prove myself all over again. I further expressed that: "If I am to prove myself over again, it would have to be somewhere other than TVA."

By accepting the RIF, I became vested in the TVA retirement system and would be able to receive a pension beginning at age of 55. I would receive severance pay at my executive pay scale. Taylor and Willis had made this decision easy for me.

I received a response to my letter from Willis saying that TVA was not asking me to prove myself. He said that: "I was one of TVA's proven managers who had a reputation for getting the job done." He went on to say that the job being offered to me, "has very significant implications for the future of TVA." He finished the letter by stating that he felt it was in my best interest to accept the job offer.

I responded by feeding his words back to him. I expressed that I appreciated the assessment of me being, "a proven manager who has a reputation for getting the job done." I told him that I was impressed that he felt that the job being offered had, "very significant implications for the future of TVA." I further stated that: "I failed to understand how someone as capable as you represented me to be in his letter could be asked to take a demotion to do something you deemed to be so important."

I again respectfully declined his job offer. Believing that this was an excellent case for a racial discrimination complaint, I went to the TVA EEO office and filed a formal action naming Willis and the Board of Directors as the discriminating officials. The way Taylor handled this by getting Willis involved made my compliant more impactful. It also meant I did not have to go after her. I felt that once the information regarding the compliant reached Willis and the Board, they would have the option of going after Taylor for getting them named as discriminating officials.

This raises a couple of questions. First, do I think that Willis's actions were discriminatory? I will allow you the reader to draw your own conclusion. Secondly, do I feel that Willis is a racist based on his role in the process of offering me a demotion? The answer is, no. At that time, and I still feel the same thirty plus years later, Willis was caught up in the culture of TVA that prevented African-American males from advancing beyond the entry level executive positions. Willis was fully aware of my capabilities; however, he was simply unwilling and lacked the courage to take a stand in my situation. He was more comfortable supporting his management team over me. He chose "comfort over conviction." Again, I thank God for giving me the wisdom and understanding to know the difference between being discriminatory and being a racist.

During the 30-day notice period, I had the sense that most felt I would change my mind. This included a number of individuals and surprisingly, even some African-Americans. One African-American individual pulled me off to the side to tell me that I was the most stubborn person he had ever met. He said I was doing some great things at TVA, and I would eventually work my way back into the executive ranks. Of course, this was a big decision. And I had no doubt that it was time for me to leave. I felt this is what God wanted me to do. I received confirmation of this when shopping at a book store. In the process of paying for the item I came to purchase, I noticed a placard on the counter next to the cash register. It had a quote by author John Gray which stated: "Success is not doing what others consider to be great, but being able to do what you deem to be right." I purchased the placard and it still sits on top of my bookcase in my home office. This is another example of the subliminal communication between God and one of His faithful followers.

On the final day of my official employment at TVA, I was in the process of packing my things when EEO Assistant Director Frank Robinson called me. He asked if I was really planning to leave. I told him that I had no option other than the RIF. He told me that if I left, TVA would be without an African-American male executive. I reminded him that should I stay, TVA would still be without an African-American male executive since I was being demoted one grade below the executive pay grade.

At this point, I learned the real purpose of his call. He then asked me if TVA made me a job offer at my current level would I consider staying. My response was I would consider such an offer if it contained a job description that had substance and allowed me to continue to have a positive impact on TVA. I told him it was not about the money at this point. The conditions of the Reduction-in-Force allowed my current salary to be frozen until my pay schedule at the lower grade caught up to M-8 level. It was about respect and dignity. He asked to come over to discuss this matter further, and I agreed.

Robinson said he could not believe I would leave. Then I asked, given how I had been treated, why I would want to stay? I am convinced that he was fishing and had I agreed, I could have remained at TVA at the executive level. Later that day, I walked out of the TVA office complex fully committed to my decision to leave and discover what God had planned for me next. As I walked to the 12th floor elevators for the final time, my thoughts went to Dad and the decision to leave his employment with the Powell Smith family and return to Lynch to work in the coal mine. I felt that he would have been very proud of his son for taking a similar stand.

The EEO complaint I filed against Willis and the Board of Directors was processed internally with no resolution. I found a local attorney who specialized in labor law. Tony Farmer and I went over my case and he agreed to represent me on a contingency basis, meaning he would not charge me an hourly fee and would only get paid if we were successful in our filing in federal court. Attorneys only take cases on a contingency basis when they feel strongly about its merits. I was responsible for payments related to the discovery aspect of the case, which included court recorder expenses, associated with taking depositions from the key players named in the suit. I did receive a degree of satisfaction when we deposed the key TVA managers involved in the process of my termination. They all contradicted each other regarding the factors that lead to the decision to not consider me for the Manager of the Personnel, Labor Relations, and EEO position. As stated earlier, TVA had historically claimed that due to the technical nature of its organization, minority and women executives were difficult to place into top echelon positions. In this case, TVA had a high ranking executive position in the administrative arena and they selected an engineering manager for the position.

The suit was heard in Knoxville's Federal District Court before an administrative judge. A jury trial was not available under guidelines at the time of my case filing in 1989. The 1964 Civil Rights Act was amended to allow for jury trials in such cases after 1991. Farmer and I were both surprised to learn that the administrative judge ruled in TVA's favor. I immediately placed this chapter in my past, knowing the outcome was also destined by God.

One of the consolations of leaving TVA were the two letters I received from personnel officers I had worked with and, in one case, supervised. Lillian Holsaple, was involved with my career as a personnel officer from my days at the Tellico Dam Project. She served on my staff when I became Chief of Management Planning for Engineering Design and Construction. In her letter, dated April 15, 1985, she wrote: "I have learned much from you. I also think our working together taught some lessons to others – not the least of which was that a black man could be the best supervisor a white woman ever had during her 42 years of working." She went on to say: "I appreciate your willingness to stand up for what was right even when it may not have been popular, and that I could rely on your taking that approach."

The other letter, dated June 27, 1984, was from Bobby Cooke, a personnel officer stationed in Chattanooga. In her letter, she wrote: "These days are tough and it especially bothers me to see people like you who have worked long and hard and distinguished themselves leave TVA. But it is TVA's loss since you will do well wherever you go." Bobby added: "I think you would be surprised, and I hope pleased, to know the number of people who I have heard express concern over you leaving. This support is well deserved."

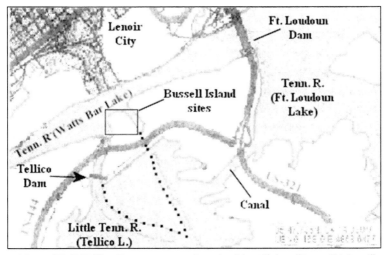

Map of TVA Tellico Dam construction site identifying "Bussell Island"
Wikipedia Public Domain

Division of Construction Personnel Services Staff
(with Supervisor Dow Murphy front row center)

College & University Placement Office Directors Tour TVA's Sequoyah Nuclear
Plant Construction site (Summer 1980)

College Recruitment Student Group Tour at TVA's Sequoyah Nuclear Plant
Construction site (Fall 1980)

Assistant Manager of TVA Office of Engineering Design and Construction (1982)

Captain Louis James Boston in Vietnam (1966)

Reverend (now Major) Louis James Boston presides over
our wedding on June 30, 1973

Wedding Photo with Karen's parent Lizzie Jones, Alfred Jones and Mom

Newly Weds at University of Tennessee married student housing

Celebrating 40th wedding anniversary with Rev. Boston
at his First Baptist Church in Annapolis, Maryland (June 30, 2013)

Life After "That Good Government Job"

P rior to leaving TVA, Karen and I had purchased a vacant commercial building in downtown Knoxville. Built in the 1800s it was located on Market Square, a retail plaza across the street from the TVA headquarters building. The City of Knoxville was in the process of investing in a major public works improvement project as part of an overall strategy of revitalizing the downtown area. Market Square was their first choice of emphasis.

We planned to open a retail establishment and take advantage of the city's efforts. Karen had spent some time at the East Tennessee Historical Society reviewing the history of the building. We discovered that we could have the building placed on the historical register and qualify for tax incentives to restore the building's original façade.

We contracted with a local architectural firm that produced a design that met the standards of the State historical group responsible for approving restoration plans. With that approval, we borrowed the $100,000 for the construction and renovations with the building as security. When construction was complete, we were able to get a 25 percent tax credit on our federal income tax for that year.

Our goal was to open a retail entertainment center. During that time, a new industry was evolving with the introduction of the video cassette recorder and the ability to rent and view prerecorded movies. The VCR also allowed for the recording of television programming.

On March 5, 1985, we opened the doors of our new business venture, Sights & Sounds Inc., which included a ribbon cutting ceremony with Kyle Testerman, the Mayor of Knoxville. The local media came to cover this milestone. The media was regularly reporting the stories regarding progress the city was making in their efforts to achieve more diverse businesses in the downtown area.

In preparation for the new business venture, I had established a relationship with a sales representative from General Electric's Atlanta, Georgia distribution center. General Electric had a division dedicated to home entertainment equipment including the VCR, televisions, audio stereo systems, and video cameras. We were able to open with a wide range of inventory representing each of these products. In addition, we had a large investment in pre-recorded video cassettes for rental and sale. This made us a complete home entertainment business.

We were the only entertainment equipment sales and video rental store located downtown. There were over 19,000 people living or working in the overall downtown area, and the store was within a block of the TVA corporate headquarters. When I developed my business plan, I thought the TVA headquarters would be an asset. There were 5,000 plus TVA employees in the immediate downtown area and many of them knew me from my work there.

As it turns out, the TVA connection was not an asset at all. It seems that a number of former co-workers perceived my leaving "that good government job" as a big mistake and predicted I would be a failure with this new retail adventure. One of the ways of making their prediction a reality was to not support the business. A coach of a softball team made up of African-American TVA employees said the team wanted to raffle off a new VCR as part of a fundraising effort and the team actually voted not to buy it from Sights & Sounds. He purchased the VCR from me despite the team's objections.

There were a number of employees adversely affected by the reorganization that lead to my departure. Some were asked to transfer to other plant sites or to Chattanooga on very short notice. One employee came by the store at around 9:00 a.m. to inform me that his supervisor had just told him that he needed to be at the Sequoyah Nuclear Plant construction site—a hundred miles from Knoxville—for a meeting at three o'clock that afternoon. He was also informed that he should be prepared to stay there and work seven days a week. This employee indicated this was the reason a lot of my former TVA coworkers were upset with me. They, too, wanted to quit due to these changing working conditions, but did not have the courage that I had exhibited. He went on to say it was difficult for his fellow white workers to accept that an African-American man was able to do something like leave a "good paying government job" and strike out on his own. I did not understand the level of resentment directed towards me; however, I had been down this road before. People had predicted I would not graduate from college. My faith had indicated I had done the right thing when I left TVA and when you have God in your corner, you don't ever have to look back.

Before opening the store, I was at Cat's Records to purchase a music CD. Ed Smith was a young African-American college student who was very impressive and the only employee in the store. Obviously, the owners had a lot of confidence in him. I immediately offered him a job to become manager at Sights & Sounds. My goal was to minimize my financial exposure by finding employment for myself and let the store be its own profit center. It wasn't realistic at this stage of the business to rely on it for personal family income.

I found a consulting job with the MAXIMA Corp. This Washington, D.C. based African-American owned company was a subcontractor to Martin-Marietta Co. in Oak Ridge, Tennessee. Martin-Marietta's contract was with the U.S. Department of Energy Oak Ridge Operations. The MAXIMA Corp. wanted to establish a unique business model with a historically black college or university. The company chose Knoxville College.

I developed a charter for the new corporation—KC/MX, Inc. (KC for Knoxville College and MX for MAXIMA). With donated computer equipment from Martin-Marietta, we were able to establish a lab for KC/MX to introduce the KC students to data entry. We had a goal of contracting their data entry skills out to companies in the area. There was also a component where KC/MX was offered a half a million dollar office supply contract with TVA.

Despite our best efforts, KC/MX never got off the ground. The way the corporation was structured, Knoxville College was a 51 percent partner. As such, they had the obligation to provide for 51 percent of the start-up capital for the business. This was critical in achieving the TVA contract. Knoxville College's financial deficits prevented them from getting the necessary line of credit to finance the TVA contract. During this time of start-up, MAXIMA assumed full responsibility for my consulting fees. Naturally, they had to sever ties with me when it was determined that the KC/MX model was no longer viable.

Knoxville College indicated that they had the resources to offer me a consulting contract to serve as acting business manager for the institution. I accepted their offer at a lower fee, with the goal that I could somehow make a contribution to help turn this struggling college around.

While working as a consultant at KC, we had to face the reality that Sights & Sounds was not going to be successful. This was at the eighteen month anniversary of the opening. I had committed to an eighteen month run and would evaluate the business at that point.

My contract with General Electric allowed me to purchase equipment on what the industry referred to as the "floor plan." This meant I could order equipment, have it available in the store, and pay for it at the time it sold. Typical floor plans allows for a six-month window, after which I would have to pay for or finance the inventory. At the time that I decided to go out of business, I called the General Electric account manager in Atlanta and informed him of my dilemma. He said he would dispatch a representative from his office to come to Knoxville, meet with me and take an inventory of their assets in the store.

Two days later the representative and I met and went over the inventory. Some of the product was out of the box on display. Some had been on the floor for the purposes of performing demonstrations and the balance was in the original boxes in the storage room. The representative indicated that Atlanta would be in touch with me and let me know the outcome of our punch list.

Devine intervention became a part of this process. The General Electric inventory was valued at $80,000. The district manager called to offer me a deal. He said if I paid the cost of shipping the equipment back to their Atlanta warehouse, he would give me 100 percent credit for the inventory. I questioned him regarding the opened boxes used for display and demonstration. He said those would be included in the 100 percent credit also, and I should merely label those boxes "display and/or demo." General Electric would repackage and distribute them to other retailers as refurbished units at a discount.

He then thanked me for being open and honest about my situation. He indicated that history had shown that retailers would file for bankruptcy and the courts would have the equipment tied up and unavailable to General Electric for the duration of the litigation. Because of my integrity, it was very easy for them to work this matter out with an ultimate win-win for the both of us. Ed Smith and I loaded the equipment in a rental van at a total cost of $120.00 and he made the one day roundtrip to Atlanta. Ironically, I chose the Monday of the federal Columbus Day holiday to make this move because of the limited activity with TVA and the banks being closed.

We still maintained the movie rental business until I could find another client to lease the building. On the following Tuesday, the customers returned to an empty store with only the movies on the shelves. One of the first customers of the day came in and blurted out: "What happened to all of your equipment?" Curiosity forced Smith to look directly at me to see what response I would give. I turned to the customer and said everyone was off yesterday and unfortunately you missed our "Columbus Day Clearance". Ed immediately excused himself to the office to avoid laughing while the customer was still standing before me.

In a relatively short period of time, I was contacted by a clothing dealer to lease the space for a retail store. We signed a contract and I found another location for the movie rental business. I applied for a new business charter for Act One Movie Rentals and relocated to a small shopping center across from the University of Tennessee's married student housing complex in West Knoxville. The building that I leased belonged to a family that was operating James' Food Market next door. When I signed the lease one of the sons of the owner said that he had considered opening a movie rental business in the space himself. My movie inventory, with depreciation, was valued at about $20,000.

Smith continued to operate the store for me. Other movie rental businesses had offered to purchase my inventory for a maximum of $5,000. I refused. This turned out to be the best option for me. After about six months, the son of the building owner approached me regarding buying my business which consisted of the movies and a customer list. I gave him a price of $25,000. We negotiated a final price of $22,500.

I was officially out of the retail business. I had managed to survive this with limited financial impact. One of the smartest moves I made was setting Sights & Sounds, Inc. up as a Sub-Chapter S Corporation. This meant that any profits or losses would be filed as a part of my personal income taxes. For IRS purposes, this was a decision companies had to make at the beginning of each fiscal year. I knew not to expect a profit in the first couple of years and was able to take the business losses on my personal income tax returns. I had escaped without having to file for bankruptcy.

The challenge I had was to keep a client in our building. The clothing retailer did not enjoy success and closed. As a result of my work and affiliation with the TVA Employees Credit Union, I had secured financing for the building renovations with them. When the clothing retailer closed, the credit union indicated that they were expanding and needed some temporary space until they could relocate to a larger downtown building to accommodate their entire operations. The credit union leased the space for about eighteen months. Recognizing the credit union lease was short term, I listed the building with a realtor for sell, but I did not have success with this effort. The building was eventually foreclosed which forced me into bankruptcy.

Recently I came across the article "Acknowledging God's Sovereignty" by author John MacArthur. In this article I was drawn to a statement that began: "The genius of Joseph's faith was his understanding the role that present circumstances play in fulfilling future promises. He accepted his blessing and adversity alike because he knew that God would use both to accomplish greater things in the future."[14]

This interpretation of the scripture can best describe how my faith allowed me to maintain a good attitude throughout the failure of Sights & Sounds and the eventual loss of the building. To this point, my journey with God had revealed that He will introduce obstacles in your life as an indication that He wants you to move in a different direction. I had to constantly remind people that the business not succeeding did not represent a failure on my part. I believe it would have been a failure had I not attempted the endeavor. How else could God continue to fulfill His promise to me?

I learned through this process, that God was preparing me for things to come. As a result of my business venture, I became a member of the Knoxville Chamber of Commerce. As a business leader, I was selected for the second class of Leadership Knoxville in 1986. I was also asked to serve my alma mater as a member of The University of Tennessee's Chancellor Associates which was an informal advisory council for Chancellor Jack E. Reese. These associations would prove very beneficial to me down the road.

As I mentioned earlier, we had to file for bankruptcy. Upon hiring a lawyer to guide us through the process, a number of things happened resulting from divine intervention. Mom had put up a $10,000 certificate of deposit to secure a loan for my business. I was able to pay off this loan and returned the certificate to her. Then the attorney told me the bankruptcy court would in all likelihood challenge the repayment of this debt and make it a part of the bankruptcy filing. Basically, the courts would not allow me to determine which debts I chose to payoff. This certainly became a major concern for me.

Going through the process, I learned that the courts had a time limit to hear and resolve all matters regarding the bankruptcy issues. The courts appoint a lawyer to represent them in the litigation of these matters. The first attorney the courts appointed, recused himself because he knew me. After about three months, the courts appointed a second attorney with the same result.

This happened a third time and the bankruptcy case was closed without being litigated, so Mom's CD was no longer was an issue. It was through these various organizations that I was able to meet and work with the three attorneys who recused themselves.

With all that had happened, I have to look back at an experience I had within a week of Sights & Sounds officially closing. I still maintained a presence downtown as I worked with the new clothing tenant. I had an interesting encounter on the Square with a former TVA co-worker. She came over and gave me a hug and with tears in her eyes, told me she was so disappointed that my business was not successful. She looked up at me and realized I had a smile on my face. This is when I informed her that God had dealt me a lot of cards up to this point in my life. When I take the business failure, this one bad card, and put it back in the deck, it gets lost. This is when she smiled and said: "James, you're going to be OK."

Hitting the Glass Ceiling

I was once on panel representing a small minority-owned business. The other panelists were mostly from Fortune 500 companies. One of the questions asked by the audience of summer African-American college interns was: "Does a glass ceiling exist in corporate America for African-Americans in 1998?" Several of the panel members including an African-American female vice president and a white female vice president, quickly pointed to their achievement and denied that a glass ceiling existed. My response to the student was that: "There is in fact a glass ceiling in corporate America today. However, if you never hit one, your question becomes mute." The problem with the preverbal glass ceiling is that, in many cases, it becomes a justification for not trying to live up to your full potential by challenging the system. Your goal should be to work hard and if you hit the glass ceiling, take your talents elsewhere.

I found it interesting that the two VP's on the panel were both female. African-American males often get left out of the equation due to the way affirmative action is perceived. If a company hires or promotes an African-American female, they get diversity credit for having both an African-American and a female. That is why African-American women and white women have benefitted more from affirmative action than African-American males in America. White females were not a part of the original Civil Rights Act of 1964. Women were added by the Democratic Party to encourage the northern faction of their party to vote against the bill which had strong Republican support. Their theory for adding women was based on the strong opposition from organized labor regarding women participating in the workforce.

The sponsors of this provision were hopeful that it would encourage the Bill's supportive northern Democratic factions to vote against it.

I had the opportunity to accept a director level position with an up-and-coming communications company. It was a position I originally turned down when I was interviewed by its president, Nick Glover.

Glover and I had met when we were members of Leadership Knoxville. Leadership Knoxville started with its first class in 1985 with a goal of getting a diverse group of local community leaders including corporate executives, non-profit executives, high level government officials, and religious leaders to become more aware of pressing issues in the community.

During this time, God provided divine intervention on two separate occasions within a six-month period. After my business venture had failed, I remained in negotiations with two local banks who had the confidence in my project to provide me with unsecured signature loans. My goal at the time was to repay these loans over an extended period of time.

Six months earlier, I had accepted a job with an Alexandria, Virginia-based company. TRESP & Associates was a minority female-owned company selected for a project in Oak Ridge, Tennessee, with the U.S. Department of Energy. I was hired as the firm's director of corporate relations. My initial assignment was to help the company get established in the Oak Ridge community by finding office space and attending community functions. The company had hired Hank Sauer as manager of the Oak Ridge office. Sauer had direct experience as a former DOE supervisor in the area for which TRESP was providing support.

You might ask: How did an Alexandria, Virginia-based company find me in Knoxville, Tennessee? Do you remember Malcolm Branner, who replaced me as supervisor of recruitment services at TVA? I had pulled some strings to get him promoted to the appropriate salary range for his position against opposition from an acting Director of Personnel. Branner had left TVA and moved to Washington, D.C. where his new wife lived and worked, and he was hired as TRESP's Human Resources Director. Upon winning the Oak Ridge contract, it was evident TRESP needed someone from the area who knew the lay of the land. It did not take Branner long to pick up the phone to assess my interest. I was invited to Alexandria for an interview and was offered the aforementioned job. The position was appealing to me because at the time I was still working as a business consultant for Knoxville College which was not able to pay my normal consultant fees.

Six months later and three years after Nick Glover and I had participated in Leadership Knoxville, I was in downtown Knoxville meeting with one of my bankers regarding a business loan. (Note: There were two signature business loans which were eventually adjudicated after I had to file bankruptcy. As a result, I did not have to pay them.)

As I was headed to my car around lunch time, I passed Glover and three of his fellow Whittle Communications executives. He and I briefly shook hands and continued on our way.

A week later, Glover somehow tracked me down. His secretary called and asked if I was available to come to Knoxville to meet with him regarding a possible opportunity at Whittle. I agreed and we set a time for the following week.

I had been reading a lot about this start-up company of creative geniuses and the call from Glover peaked my interest. How would someone with my skill set fit in with a company focusing on publishing?

Glover began the interview by telling me that Whittle Communications had been approached by the Summit Leadership Coalition (SLC). The African-American activists were approaching Knoxville-based companies to encourage them to improve their diversity by hiring more African-Americans. Glover said he and Chris Whittle, board chairman and founder, recognized they had not done enough in this area and were receptive to the goals of the Summit Leadership Coalition.

He said they had interviewed a number of candidates suggested by SLC to lead their efforts; however, none of the candidates were appealing to Whittle. He wanted me to consider taking the position of Whittle's Equal Employment Opportunity Director.

I immediately thanked Glover for considering me. However, I respectfully declined. I explained to him that in corporate America, minorities are historically placed in director and executive position relating to achieving diversity and rarely are given the opportunity to impact the company's bottom line. I told him I had made a commitment to myself to never get pigeon-holed into one of these EEO positions.

A couple of days later, Glover's secretary called me again and asked if I would consider coming back to Whittle and meet with Glover and Chris Whittle. I agreed.

In the meeting with Glover and Whittle, they reiterated their desire to have a more successful diversity program and they understood my reservations. Whittle told me that, based on my previous interview with Glover, I was exactly the person they were looking for to lead this effort.

My response again was to discourage them from hiring me. I told Chris that his commitment to the Summit Leadership Coalition would not be well received when they learned that Whittle Communications had chosen me to be the program's director. The problem was that my views on achieving diversity was diametrically opposite to theirs. I said I did not believe in the establishment of goals and timetables because in most cases they established unrealistic expectations for the company and the community as well. Furthermore, I noted, the director of EEO has no authority to hire and effect the company's diversity numbers.

In response to this, they asked me what would be my approach. I told them the only way diversity would work was to integrate the concept into the culture of the company and hold the hiring divisions and departments accountable for success or failure. Should I take the job, I would want a travel budget to take senior editors and managers to minority journalism conferences. I wanted the money in my budget to ensure that departments could not use budgetary constraints as a basis for not participating. This would be in addition to an advertising budget for periodicals and exhibit booths at annual conferences. Each of the targeted minority groups—National African-American Journalist Association, Asian-America Journalist Association, Hispanic Journalist Association and Native American Journalist Association—held annual conferences at different locations throughout the country and in the case of the Hispanic association, in Puerto Rico.

The other issue I emphasized was that the major publishing and media companies were working to increase the pool of minority candidates through academic scholarships. I felt if Whittle was going to be a player in this arena, minority and women scholarships had to be a part of the mix. Whittle and Glover later committed to five full-ride minority and women scholarships annually with the University of Tennessee's College of Journalism.

From a staffing standpoint, I would only need a secretary. They were impressed to hear this. Glover said that one candidate they interviewed requested a staff of 25. Whittle then asked me, what was my bottom line? I told him that my goal would be to work myself out of a job in two to two and half years.

They obviously came prepared to get a commitment from me. They made me an offer at the director level (an increase of $25,000 over what I was making at TRESP), and the opportunity to purchase 5,000 shares in the limited partnership. In addition, they agreed to all of my previous demands regarding budgets and indicated that since I was not comfortable with director of Equal Employment Opportunity title, I could come up with my own title. We immediately settled on Director of Community Relations and Diversity.

This all took place as a result of the previous business failure. Had I not been downtown meeting with the banker, the encounter with Glover would never have taken place and it would have been a matter of out of sight, out of mind. This was obvious divine intervention.

I literally hit the ground running, establishing reservations for the aforementioned conferences and lining up the senior editors who had openings, to attend with me. We established an information booth and the editors attended some of the workshops. At mealtime, I would purposely disappear until the ballroom where the meal was being served was full. Entering the ballroom, I would immediately notice our Whittle editors at tables introducing themselves and exchanging business cards. They were now establishing their own contacts and in the future would not need me as an intermediary. I love it when a plan comes together.

I did encounter some road blocks along the way. The SLC members happened to be gathered at a local night spot where a friend and I would go have a beer after playing basketball at the downtown YMCA. Upon spotting me, about five of them decided to surround our table, even bringing their chairs. They informed me that they were responsible for getting me the job at Whittle, and that they had certain expectations of me. I told them that I would be interested in what they had to say; however, I said that I did not work for them. One of the members immediately stepped up and told me they had gotten me the job, and they could get it taken away. My response was that if they could get my job, then I really don't have a job. I also told them I had a job prior to joining Whittle and finding a job had not been that difficult for me in the past. This conversation did not go well.

Two days later, Whittle summoned me to his office. He had apparently been in discussion with the SLC regarding the encounter at the night club. He indicated that they accused me of being arrogant. This is when I reminded Whittle that the SLC would not be pleased with his selection of me for the position. I also indicated to Whittle that as an African-American man, people who like you consider you to be self-confident and those who dislike you consider you to be arrogant. I reiterated to him that I would not achieve anything that would be pleasing in their sight because of differences in approach. I do not think Chris was necessarily pleased with the response he received from me; however, I think he understood.

My problems with the African-American community did not end there. When my plans to increase diversity were finalized and approved by Whittle, I established a meeting with the Summit Leadership Coalition to give them an update. Fortunately for me, I was wise enough to ask Laura Eshbaugh to attend the meeting with me. Eshbaugh handled legal matters for the partnership and was one of Whittle's most trusted partners. When they asked about goals and timetables, I informed them that there would be none. One of the participants immediately referred to the plan as a bunch of crap simply because we did not have the traditional goals and timetables. This was even before the presentation was made. Eshbaugh could not believe her ears, after what we both felt was an ambitious program including the full-ride minority and women scholarships.

Whittle would enhance his standing in the Knoxville African-American community when he announced a $5,000, five-year annual commitment to the Dr. Martin Luther King Jr. Commemoration Committee.

Next I was summoned to meet with the board of directors for the Knoxville Community Development Corporation, the community organization through which federal economic development funds were funneled. KCDC was instrumental in using some federal dollars in the development of the new downtown Whittle corporate headquarters complex. Apparently the local African-American Contractors

Association wasn't pleased with my efforts to involve minority construction contractors in the building of the headquarters. They felt that the KCDC board could exercise pressure as a result of their earlier involvement in the land acquisition.

The president of the African-American Contractors Association was Mark Deathridge, owner of East Tennessee Mechanical Contractors. It was quite apparent at the beginning of the meeting, that the KCDC board realized that their association had overestimated their ability to involve themselves in the construction process. I had read the documents pertaining to minority participation and the requirements were that Whittle, its developers, and contractors, would make every effort to involve community-based minority contractors in the construction.

Recognizing that the requirement was for local minority firm participation, I informed the KCDC board that I reached out to minority firms throughout the state of Tennessee to include Knoxville, Chattanooga, Nashville, and Memphis. My contacts were primarily through their NAACP chapters and National Urban League affiliates. They were invited to come to Knoxville and join local minority contractors at an information meeting where the developer, Lawler-Wood, and the prime construction contractor, Johnson and Galyon, would be present to go over the scope of the project and discuss their subcontractor requirements. Johnson and Galyon also brought some of their traditional principal subcontractors who could use additional support.

One of the interesting things about this process was that the African-American Contractors Association had become accustomed to dealing with the federal contracting process, where they had to be a 51 percent participant in order to qualify for minority contracting opportunities. Ironically, during my presentation at the aforementioned meeting with the minority contractors present, I was able to introduce them to the private sector concept of allowing them to team with major subcontractors without the 51 percent requirement. My thinking was that if they could get, for example, 20 percent and the majority company gained the other 80 percent, there was nothing wrong with that arrangement. The African-American Contractor Association's response was that they expected us to package work for them and let them determine if it would be productive for them to participate. My response was that the way we proposed to proceed would not place limits on how large of the pie they could handle. I did not want to make the mistake of slicing the pie and getting them upset because the package sent to them was too small. Only the minority contractors knew of their ability to respond. Overall, the meeting ended with the KCDC board being impressed with my approach, which was more than they could have expected.

One of the member companies with the African-American Contractors Association teamed with a local excavation company to haul dirt from the construction site. His share of the contract was 20 percent of $300,000. He was to receive $60,000 for hauling dirt from the site. A problem with a buried fuel tank resulted in the contract being amended to $500,000 and his efforts were rewarded with another $40,000.

I achieved success in other areas with minority-owned businesses. Frances Hall, owner of Hall & Associates, exclusively handled all of my promotional advertising. Hall & Associates was a minority woman-owned company that provided graphic arts and creative design services.

When Whittle launched *Channel One*, its ten minute news program for school systems across the country, there were opportunities for subcontractors to install the satellite equipment for receiving the daily broadcasts and setting up the television monitors throughout the schools. Whittle had established a prime contract with an Atlanta, Georgia-based company for the overall installation project. Their plans were to subcontract most of the installation with local companies in the areas where Whittle had established contracts for *Channel One.*

I made a trip to Atlanta to meet with the owners of this company. I was accompanied by David Andrews, of Knoxville minority-owned and operated Andrews Electric. Andrews was successful in getting a number of installation contracts throughout the Southeast.

Needless to say, things were going well, until I got caught up in a company reorganization. Chris Whittle had hired Tom Ingram, his former public relations consultant into a full-time vice president position. By this time Glover had left the company and I was reporting to Eshbaugh who wanted me to continue reporting to her. She had attended some community meetings with me and was able to witness first hand some of the unwarranted hostility directed at me by some of the African-American community leaders. She also understood that I was achieving the type of success they had envisioned when they hired me.

A prime example was when Whittle rolled out its *Channel One,* the morning television program for middle and high schools, they did not envision the level of resistance they would receive because of the two minutes of advertising shown during the ten-minute daily broadcast. Some parents and elected school board officials were not enthusiastic. Whittle had another problem with their marketing model. They hired fresh college graduates who were mostly white and sent them into urban areas such as Pittsburg, Chicago, and Los Angeles. These white 20-somethings were not prepared to make presentations to school boards that included a number of African-Americans, with some serving as chairpersons. In a school board meeting in Pittsburg, a Whittle representative was asked: "How many minorities did Whittle employ?" The female rep respondent by asking: "What difference does that make?" The African-American chairman retorted: "If you do not understand that question, you do not need to be making a presentation to this board." He immediately went to the next agenda item. Eshbaugh asked the young lady to come to my office for guidance on how to get this back on track. I picked up the phone and called the chairman. Following an apology, I introduced myself and shared with him the exciting things we were achieving at Whittle. I also told him of the diversity in the Channel One programming and informed him that our chief anchor was Mark Carter, an African-American Harvard graduate. He agreed to place Channel One on a future agenda.

Eshbaugh had a greater appreciation for my contribution when I attended the National Black Educators Association meeting in Dallas, Texas. Lynn Vogel was the public relations liaison for educational related programs, including *Channel One.* Vogel, being a white female apparently was not comfortable attending such a majority African-American function. She asked Eshbaugh to send me to represent Whittle and introduce *Channel One* to this captive audience. I agreed to attend and asked one of our female African-American *Channel One* producers from New York to join me.

The trip was an overwhelming success. The producer and I were able to impress some school board members, including a junior high principal from Los Angeles County, California. They arranged for us to make a ten-minute presentation to the NBEA board of directors' meeting convening later that afternoon. We were a big hit.

The principal of a technical magnet school asked that, if she could arrange it, would I come to California and make a presentation to her school board. She thought that the technology associated with *Channel One* and its delivery system would be a perfect match for her program.

After returning, I reported our success to Eshbaugh. The principal did follow up and said the school board was going to designate a half day of school and invite board members, parents, and community educators to the presentation. At the time, Whittle Communications was getting strong resistance from the California Secretary of Education, who was threating to withhold state funds from schools signing up for Channel One. The funds withheld would be equivalent to the amount of time spent involved with Channel One. The Los Angeles County School District did not seem to be intimidated by the secretary's threat. The meeting was scheduled, and I confirmed I would fly out and be accompanied by the Whittle *Channel One* marketing rep for their area.

After all of my efforts, someone in the organization made the decision that I should not go to California. They indicated that I was not in the marketing organization, and my services were no longer needed. New boss Ingram notified me of the decision two days before I was scheduled to fly to California. I was gracious and contacted the principal at the school and told her of my change of plans. I informed her that the Whittle *Channel One* marketing representative from her area would be there to make the presentation. I took the high road recognizing the significant steps the principal had taken to give Whittle and *Channel One* exposure to her school district.

Although, I was no longer reporting to Eshbaugh, a few weeks later she informed me that as result of my contact in LA County, eight additional school districts in the area had signed up for *Channel One.*

Ingram and I did not seem to be compatible in terms of our working relationship. We discussed the possibility of me transferring to another organization within Whittle. This option proved to be unrealistic. While I would have preferred to stay with Whittle in another capacity, I informed Ingram that I would be willing to accept a severance package to leave the company as an alternative.

In the meantime, the raises for the coming year were announced. All director level and below were to receive a 2.5 percent increase. Vice presidents were to receive a 1 percent increase.

When I received my director level increase, I noticed that it was only 1 percent. I raised this question with Ingram and he said he would get back with me. This is when I discovered that when I was hired, I was placed on the VP pay scale but I was a director in title only. Therefore, I would only get a 1 percent increase.

The discriminatory impact of this decision, was that I was not a VP. Vice presidents in the company were entitled to an exceptional fringe benefits package. It included an annual car allowance, first-class air travel, and stays at luxury hotel suites. As you might image, the VP's were practically all driving, Audi's, BMW's, Porsche's, and Mercedes.

Ingram did come back with a very lucrative severance package and I was able to bid Whittle good-bye. This was a first for me, an entry level job that represented the glass ceiling.

My relationship with Whittle Communications took an interesting turn some eighteen months later. When I left in July 1992, I decided to write a book about the flaws associated with affirmative action and how, in most cases, it was a concept that was not necessarily positive for the African-American community. Although we have had successes, many of the practices associated with affirmative action were discriminatory in implementation. I wanted to discuss the model I introduced at Whittle of integrating diversity into the culture of the company by holding the managers accountable. Too many companies make the mistake of establishing EEO officers and attempt to make them responsible for the success or failure of the programs. A person who does not hire or fire people can't be held accountable for something outside of their control.

I completed the manuscript in late December 1993 and mailed it to a journalist acquaintance to edit for me. It was never published.

At the beginning of January 1994, on the very day that my wife and children returned to school following the Christmas holiday break, I found myself with no job and essentially nothing to do. Out of the blue, the telephone rang. It was Jeff Wood, a friend I met on the basketball courts at the YMCA, where a group of us played two or sometimes three times a week.

Wood and an associate, Basil Skelton, had formed a new company called Solutions to Environmental Problems. After sharing the concept behind STEP, he said his partner needed to ask me a question. Wood had told him that I had previously worked at Whittle Communications. Skelton was trying to get corporate sponsorships for his son's hockey team and wanted to know the best person to contact at Whittle. I gave him the name and telephone number of the person who assumed my duties in community relations. This is when divine intervention became a part of the conversation.

Basil reiterated that he and Wood were starting this new firm and needed help with some administrative details, and wanted to know if I would be interested in working on a consultant contract with them. I gave him my standard fee, and he asked me to come in the next day and we could put a contract together. Again, the irony was it was the Whittle Communications connection that lead to the telephone call from Wood, resulting in Skelton offering me the consultant opportunity. The dots keep on being connected.

Becoming a Project Manager

The experience at Solutions to Environmental Problems was one of ups and downs. As with many start-up companies, funding was always a challenge. STEP was considered a minority-owned company because Jeff Wood, an African-American was a 51 percent owner. Basil Skelton and Michael Palmer shared the 49 percent balance. One of the problems I had right off the bat was that Skelton had encouraged Wood to learn how to play golf. He felt that more deals could be made on the golf course and Wood needed to be able to join him should the opportunity present itself. My problem was that Wood would invite me to go play golf with him during normal work hours on a regular basis. It did not look good that the two African-Americans were out playing golf while the whites were working. Tammy, the company's white female administrative assistant, seemed to resent this more than anyone. As a result, she built up a long-term antagonistic attitude towards me throughout my tenure at STEP, knowing that she could not get Wood fired since he was company president.

Despite my playing golf with Wood, I was still able to make a contribution. I assisted in the development of STEP's application to participate in the U.S. Small Business Administration's Section 8(a) Program. This was the program that allowed for federal agencies to set-a-side specific contracts exclusively for minority and women owned firms. Without the certification from the SBA, firms did not qualify to participate. This process generally takes a year to eighteen months.

In the meantime, I was able to assist Skelton in securing a contract with TVA to provide the environmental monitoring for one of their coal fired steam plant's ash ponds.

The SBA rejected STEP's application for the Section 8(a) Program due to questions regarding an initial investment by Science Applications International Corporation. Skelton was employed by SAIC prior to becoming a partner in STEP. SBA determined this affiliation was suspicious regarding the impact of ownership and their upfront investment. STEP had to wait a year to reapply. This proved to be a major set-back for STEP and my contract was terminated, which was a prudent business decision.

I ended up taking a job working on the assembly line at the local Panasonic production plant, which manufactured automobile speakers for a group of car manufactures. I was there for about six weeks when Wood again gave me a call.

They needed my assistance regarding a legal matter with U.S. Department of Labor. Someone had filed a complaint that STEP was in violation of the Fair Labor Standards Act. The issue was STEP's policy regarding payment of overtime to its employees. Skelton and Wood were very confident their process was good in that it allowed STEP to still keep employees on the payroll even during times when they could not provide work for them. To balance this out, the company was banking the overtime money they were receiving from their clients and paying the workers the straight time hourly rate rather than the time-and-a half they were entitled to receive.

With my human resources background, I was very familiar with FLSA and immediately recognized that STEP was in violation. STEP placed me on the payroll again to help them navigate this process. I met with the local U. S. Department of Labor office, introduced myself and indicated that I was in agreement with their assessment. They were pleased to hear this, as the initial reaction they had received from STEP, in their opinion, was combative and uncooperative.I went to the meeting with a proposal for resolving the matter. I recommended to them I would conduct an internal audit of STEP's payroll, identify the individuals who were deserving of the overtime, and report my findings back to them. Knowing that these offices oftentimes do not have the manpower to conduct such audits in a timely fashion, I was able to convince Wood and Skelton that this was the best approach. One, they did not want to have the Labor Department representative in their office conducting the audit. Secondly, the sooner they got this behind them the quicker we could implement the proper overtime practice for compensating the employees. The Labor Department indicated the audit would only have to go back two years due to the stature of limitations. When I completed the audit and presented the findings, the Department of Labor was pleased. They became very cooperative in minimizing the impact on STEP. There would be no fines. They also allowed STEP to make equal monthly installments over six months directly to the Labor Department, who in turn would distribute the monies to the impacted workers.

With this behind STEP, it was now time to begin the process of reapplying for the SBA Section 8(a) Program. One of the things I encouraged Wood to do was take a trip and meet with officials in the Atlanta office. We had determined that the initial application was actually rejected by the SBA Tennessee District Office in Nashville. Our suspicions were that some officials in the Oak Ridge contracting community had made a complaint with Nashville regarding the SAIC position, which resulted in their rejection. I convinced Wood the Atlanta SBA office had the option of approving or rejecting the Tennessee District's recommendation.

This proved to be critical. Wood and I met with the Atlanta SBA representative and were able to impress upon them that Wood was indeed the president of the company and STEP met all of the requirements for participation in the Section 8(a) Program. The STEP application was approved by SBA in Washington, D.C.

Prior to getting the 8(a) classification, I had met with a contracting officer for the U.S. Corps of Engineers in Huntsville, Alabama. He told me that once we received the 8(a) we should come to Huntsville and meet with him. I followed up and took Mike Palmer with me. Palmer was handling the environmental training—hazard material handling—for STEP. We were able to secure a $100,000 contract to provide training for this agency.

Things were starting to look up for STEP. Wood was continuing his habit of leaving early to go play golf; it was like he had become addicted to the sport. He asked me to attend a bi-weekly meeting on Tuesday afternoons at two o'clock for him while he played golf. Following the meeting, it would be my quitting time; therefore, I would not return to the office. As the company's human resources manager, I made it a point to be at work at 7:00 a.m. This way I would be available to the employees before they went into the field should they have any HR concerns. I would then leave at four o'clock or a little after.

Tammy, not realizing that I was attending these bi-weekly meetings for Wood, convinced Skelton that I had a habit of leaving early and implied she had to get involved with HR issues in my absence. This is when Skelton approached me and indicated I should start working from 8:00 a.m. to 5:00 p.m. I told him I would comply. He was taken aback that I did not raise any objections. He told me I could appeal his decision to Wood if I thought that he was being unfair. I told him there would be no need; that he was the company vice president and I did not have a problem with his decision. The next day, Wood came into my office to discuss what had transpired. He said Tammy was complaining regarding me leaving at 2:00 p.m. and not returning to work. This is when I reminded Wood that I had been representing him in these bi-weekly meetings with the other contractors. He asked me if I had told Skelton about the meetings when my new reporting time was discussed. I told him, no. I understood the source of his actions, and honestly, the only people penalized by the decision were the employees that I had come to work early to assist. I had no problem working from eight-to-five.

This is when divine intervention was again revealed. The STEP organization did not know I was in on-going discussion with Mark Deathridge, president of East Tennessee Mechanical Contractors for a management position with his company. Deathridge and I were having some get acquainted dinners and informational sessions regarding an upcoming contract proposal he was working on with the U.S. Department of Energy's Oak Ridge Operations. He was looking for someone to head up the proposal writing team and, if successful, to become project manager for the contract. It would take about a year to complete the process. Deathridge indicated he could offer me a guaranteed one-year contract and, should we not be successful, there would be a possibility I would have to be terminated. This meeting took place on a Monday evening. I told him to draw up the contract and I would meet with him on the following Wednesday to finalize the deal.

On Tuesday, Tammy decided she would let me know that she was responsible for my new work schedule. She entered my office and in a loud voice, where everyone could hear her, went into a rant saying over and over again, "eight to five", "eight to five." When she was finished, I politely asked her to leave my office. She did not stay long enough to see the big smile on my face. She had just helped me confirm my decision to leave STEP and take Deathridge's one year deal. God is good!

I met with Deathridge on Wednesday and we signed the contract. Thursday morning I went into Wood's office and handed him my resignation letter. He indicated that he did not want me to go. Skelton had not arrived at work at this point. Wood picked up the phone to tell him I was leaving STEP.

When Skelton arrived at work, he asked me to go to lunch with him to discuss my resignation. As with Wood, Skelton said he did not want me to go. I told him my decision was final. Further I said I did not feel the company appreciated my contribution, and I felt he had not given me his support as vice president. I pointed to the decision to change my work schedule as a prime example. He made the decision without the courtesy of asking why I was leaving early. I then told him it felt as if I was working for Tammy, since she got to determine my work schedule and that to me that was unacceptable. He then asked me what I was going to do. Without revealing my opportunity with ETMC, I told him I was a big boy and could take care of myself.

It is interesting to note that my experience at Whittle actually played a significant role in the opportunity with ETMC. Mark Deathridge was president of the African-American Contractors Association when they requested a meeting to challenge my efforts to involve minority contractors with the Whittle Communications headquarters construction effort. While the contractors association was not pleased with the outcome of the meeting, I found it interesting that Deathridge thought enough of my abilities to consider me as a candidate to come to work for his company. I later learned that Frances Hall, who I contracted with at Whittle to provide graphic design services for the recruitment advertising, was the catalyst for getting Deathridge to consider me. Working with Deathridge as a consultant, she felt that the contract was a huge undertaking and that he needed someone with a strong management background and a reputation of integrity who he could trust. ETMC was teaming with Johnson Controls Federal Services, based in Cape Canaveral, Florida on its bid to win the contract and Hall knew that Deathridge needed someone who was not easily intimidated by this large company and would protect his interest. I started to work for Deathridge after serving my two weeks' notice with STEP. ETMC was successful in its bid with DOE and I became Project Manager James B. Bussell. The dots continue to be connected.

Take Off that Nigger Baseball Cap

The Request-for-Proposal that Mark Deathridge had hired me to work on was a facilities management and maintenance contract for the U.S. Department of Energy. The contract was being performed by Johnson Controls Federal Systems based in Cape Canaveral, Florida. It appeared that the Energy Department was not totally satisfied with Johnson Controls' overall performance. DOE decided that they would revamp the contract and place it out for competitive bid exclusively among SBA-affiliated small business enterprises. This process is different from the SBA Section 8(a) process, where federal agencies could choose to sole source a contract to a qualified minority or woman-owned firm. ETMC would have to compete with other small businesses to be successful.

Due to their size, Johnson Controls no longer qualified to bid on the contract. With them eliminated from the competition, Deathridge felt his best chance for winning the bid was to select Johnson Controls as a subcontractor. They had the experience which would certainly enhance ETMC's credentials. Their knowledge of the scope of the contract would give ETMC some insight on how to best approach performing the scope of work as well as putting together the most responsive and cost competitive bid package to DOE.

Deathridge had hired me in March 1996 and during the Christmas holiday of that year, DOE informed ETMC that we had been successful with our bid of $45 million dollars over a contract period of five years. The contract was actually awarded as a three year contract, with two one year options, with a start-up date of March 1997.

Upon being awarded the contract, my first move as the project manager was to meet with the construction trades and labor union representatives to introduce myself and share with them provisions of our successful bid and how the employees they represent would be affected. A major part of our bid process was that we placed our potential profits at risk. This meant that if we did not perform to DOE's satisfaction, we would not be awarded any profit for our performance. However, if we did a good job, the fees would be doubled based on a specific formula outlined in the contract. One of the things I convinced Mark to do, was to share with the employees ten percent of any award fee ETMC received from DOE during our semi-annual evaluation periods. My thesis was that we were evaluated not only on work performance, but our safety record, our employee relations efforts, and other such items. With that being the case, the workers should share in the award profits because they were the ones who would make our success possible.

The meeting with the employee union representatives went well. I informed them that we were going to reduce the project operations from its current one hundred employees down to seventy-four. I assured them that the cuts would be across the board and would not single out the craft workers. I also mentioned the sharing of the profits. The one question they asked me, which seemed to be a major concern: Was I going to be managing the contract or was ETMC going to yield to Johnson Controls to run the show? The union representatives did not have a good working relationship with Johnson Controls when they had the contract and were somewhat apprehensive regarding their being a subcontractor for ETMC. This labor relations dilemma was one of the basis for DOE repackaging the contract and eliminating Johnson Controls from the competition.

My response was that I would be the project manager and there would be no doubt that ETMC would be in charge. The group thanked me for the meeting and giving them a heads-up on what was to be expected when ETMC took over. My goal was to empower these guys so their employees would appreciate their leadership. They gave their membership a good endorsement of ETMC.

As the new project manager, I introduced myself to the staff of one hundred. My introduction was very straight forward. My management philosophy consisted of three basis principals.

- I treat people like I wish to be treated.
- As the boss, I do not make decisions that I can't explain. If you work for me and do not understand a decision, come see me.
- Lastly, we spend most of our wakening hours at work, if you can't have fun here on the job, you can't have fun in the other aspects of your life. We are going to get the job done, and we are going to have fun in the process.

As a part of the question and answer session, I was asked about the layoffs that were forth coming and its impact on the employees in the room. As it turned out, we ended up laying off 26 employees. In terms of my initial commitment to treat employees like I wished to be treated, I informed the human resources and payroll coordinators for the project that when we issued the notifications to those affected by the reduction-in-force, I wanted the notification day to be their last. My goal was to give them their final pay check on that day, which included thirty-day's pay for the contractual notice period and any vacation pay they would accrue during the notice period. Finally, I would personally give them their notice and thank them for their service to the previous contractors.

I shared with them that their thirty-day notice period could be better spent getting their lives organized and adjusting to life after their work on this project was complete. In an effort to get on with the task at hand, I did not want the remaining employees subjected to facing their impacted co-workers every day of the thirty-day notice period.

In our contract proposal to the Department of Energy, ETMC divided the scope of work into two packages. Johnson Controls and their personnel would continue to operate and maintain the water treatment plant. This plant produced approximately thirteen million gallons of water per day and served the DOE Y-12 reservation, as well as the city of Oak Ridge. Johnson Controls employees would also maintain the two shops for vehicle and heavy equipment maintenance. ETMC and its employees were responsible for maintaining the roads and grounds for the entire footprint of the DOE reservation including grass mowing, road paving and snow removal during the winter months. We managed the warehouse and administrative support for the project.

I immediately faced a couple of challenges as the new project manager. Richard Baxter, Johnson Controls' lead manager, had difficulty recognizing that ETMC had become the prime contractor. He was a part of the previous team that represented Johnson Controls on their contract with DOE. Within the first two weeks of taking over the contract, there was a major break in the water line from the lake where we were pumping water up to the plant. Baxter decided to not inform me of the water break and sent a letter directly to our customer, DOE. I learned about the break three days later from our safety manager, Tom McMillian.

At the end of the shift, I asked Baxter to stick around for a discussion. This is when I informed him that the next time he kept me out of the loop on something like this, he may find himself on his way back to Johnson Controls' Cape Canaveral headquarters. Further I informed him that he had no authority as ETMC's subcontractor to ever contact the DOE directly, and the protocol was for all communications from this project to DOE would be through ETMC.

Baxter's response was that I was now playing "with the big boys," indicating I was out of my league since I worked for such a small outfit like ETMC. My response was he should not make the mistake of underestimating me. Frances Hall turned out to be a prophet because she saw this coming.

Following our discussion, Baxter apparently sent off an e-mail to his bosses in Florida indicating he was having difficulty with me as project manager. Apparently his e-mail infuriated his bosses and they gave him a lecture on the difference between being a prime contractor versus being a subcontractor. They indicated that they expected him to be fully cooperative with me in the future. This information was revealed to me the next morning when my secretary, Jean Hudson, came into my office and informed me that Baxter had approached her regarding helping him mend fences with me. This is when I informed Hudson I had no problems with Baxter. My discussion with him the previous day laid down my expectations and as long as he understood his role, we would not have problems in the future.

My second challenge also came during the first month. Being a new contractor, we issued employees baseball caps with the ETMC/Johnson Controls logo. One employee walked into the heavy equipment maintenance shop and was told by one of his fellow mechanics to: "Take off that 'nigger' baseball cap." I learned about the incident some two weeks after it happened. Boyd Kitts, shop supervisor, came by my office and I inquired about the "nigger baseball cap" incident. He was surprised that I had heard about it. He immediately apologized and asked me what he should do about the situation. I told him that two weeks had passed and it was a little too late to consider any kind of disciplinary action. I knew that most companies would send out a letter to all employees regarding use of racial slurs on the project. It has always been my position that it is insulting to the good employees to receive such a notice when they are not the guilty party. I informed Kitts that I would handle the situation.

After a couple of days, I went down to the shop and approached Jack, who had used the racial slur. I introduced myself and informed him that I understood he had used the word "nigger" when referring to the ETMC baseball cap. I asked him to let me finish before he said anything. I told him I was new on the job and all that I asked of him and the rest of the employees was for them to judge me based on the way I treat them. He responded that he could do that. This is when I told him, that as far as the "nigger cap" incident is concerned, it is now behind us and forgotten. As I departed, I gave Jack a tap on the shoulder to send a message to those observing that things were good between us. If Jack wanted them to know what we discussed, he would have to be the one to tell them. It did not take long for the word to spread all over the project that I had met with Jack, who became one of the biggest advocates of ETMC. When we would bring potential clients to the shops for a tour, Jack would tell them: "This is the best outfit I have ever worked for."

Unfortunately, several months later, Jack passed away suddenly while working on his farm. I attended his family visitation and was extremely pleased when his dad and son sought me out to tell me how much Jack thought of me. Jack and I had become special friends. I still have a paper weight on my desk at home that he crafted for me out of a piece of rebar steel. I thank God for giving me the wisdom to understand and seek out the best in people. The rewards are mindboggling.

At the end of our first six-month evaluation period, we sent in our response, which was a self-assessment of the DOE evaluation criteria established for our contract. We had met or exceeded the requirements and I fully anticipated a rating of 96 (outstanding) or above. We had a perfect safety record. We laid off twenty-six workers and there were no grievances filed by the unions, no complaints to the DOE personnel staff, and no Congressional inquiries. This was indicative of handling the situation in a fair, equitable, and compassionate manner.

When the DOE announced their rating, ETMC received a rating of 92 which was superior. I was disappointed and frustrated at the same time. The problem was that we had met the DOE criteria for "outstanding performance" and they did not want to recognize a minority-owned company, and its African-American project manager.

Against the advice of other DOE contractors and some of my own managers, I decided to appeal their rating for two reasons. The first reason was that we had placed our profits at risk and fully expected the customer to be fair. Secondly, the financial difference between a 92 and 96 rating was about $65,000. Thirdly, I wanted to send the message that should they be unfair during future evaluations, they should expect to see me again.

During the appeal meeting with the Marlena Clark, contracting officer for the project, I pointed out that the DOE had deducted points in the evaluation in the area related to human resources. This area dealt with the number of grievances filed during the review period. In our self-assessment ETMC had reported that there were no grievances filed.

This meant we should have received a 100 percent rating in this category, making our overall performance outstanding. Then I asked her how we could improve on a 100 percent. At this point, she knew I had presented a valid argument for a successful appeal. Her response was that they do not typically give outstanding ratings on the first evaluation period. My response to her was that DOE should include the statement: "Do not expect an outstanding rating in your first evaluation period in the contract document." That was the only reason we did not receive an outstanding rating.

A member of the DOE Human Resources Department called me to say that after their review of the HR portion of our self-evaluation, they had recommended that ETMC receive a 100 percent. What was most impressive to them was the fact that we laid off twenty-six employees and not one grievance was filled. What is appalling about this matter is that Clark is an African-American. One would think that giving a minority-owned company its due recognition of outstanding would be a matter of pride.

It is interesting to note that the American Water Works Association, Kentucky-Tennessee District awarded ETMC their Award of Excellence for Plant Operations Greater Than 10 Million Gallon Per/Day (MGD) for 1997/1998 for the DOE Water Treatment Plant. Another endorsement of our outstanding performance.

This would not be the last time I found myself protesting the treatment ETMC was receiving from persons charged with the oversight of our contract with DOE. In a budget meeting with representatives from the finance department of the DOE, the finance officer informed me that Jim Hall, manager of the DOE Oak Ridge Operations had directed her to add $250,000 to ETMC's contract to take over the maintenance of DOE-owned and operated Carbide Park. The park was a recreational area on Milton Hill Lake. Apparently, DOE's largest prime contractor, had run out of money for this specific task and asked DOE for another $250,000. Mr. Hall's response was that since ETMC was doing such an outstanding job on their facilities maintenance contract, he would prefer to turn the scope of work over to us.

George Herron, our African-American technical contracting specialist, stated that ETMC would not be receiving the funding. After the meeting adjourned, I returned to my office and gave Herron a call regarding the funding. He pulled his Caucasian supervisor, Dick Anders into our phone conversation. When I raised the question regarding not being awarded the $250,000, Anders said the reason we did not receive the money was because the contract would require ETMC to hire lifeguards for the pools during the summer months. He felt ETMC would not want to do that. My response was: "Let me get this straight. Do you mean to tell me that we can produce thirteen million gallons of water a day at the treatment plant and can't hire someone to swim in it?" Anders then told me the conversation was over and hung up.

Anders immediately called me back and said he did not appreciate the tone of my response. He suggested we have lunch the next day to discuss my attitude towards him. I agreed, and he gave me a place and time.

The next day we met at the designated location. He began by telling me he did not appreciate my response the day before. I told him he was certainly not going to like my attitude that day either. Then

I asked: "How can you sleep at night, knowing that you took $250,000 out of a small, local, minority-owned business's budget and gave it to an international conglomerate where the amount is so small that it doesn't even show up on their radar screen?"

Needless to say, Anders did not have an answer and he sat there quietly for the balance of the lunch. As we picked up our separate checks, I heard him mumble that this was the worse lunch he had ever had.

It was these types of confrontations that I knew would eventually lead to my wearing out my welcome with the Department of Energy and its oversight staff. As a project manager, I understood the implications for Deathridge and ETMC. While the Energy Department knew that my assertions were correct, I purposely would not involve Deathridge in my confrontations. Deathridge was well liked by the DOE brass and it was easier to blame me. When I made them mad, they would call him and complain about me. I knew he had the opportunity to exercise options of two more years, once the first three years of the contract were completed. My protest had an impact in that we received a 95 superior rating during the second sixth month evaluation period and outstanding ratings for the balance of the contract.

In the last year of the three-year contract, I convinced Deathridge to approach Johnson Controls corporate management in Florida about purchasing their interest in the contract. We would make a lump sum payment and place the Johnson Controls employees on ETMC's payroll. This would give ETMC 100 percent control of the contract. Johnson Controls surprisingly accepted the proposal and ETMC ended up taking over the two maintenance shops and operation and maintenance of the water treatment plant.

My parting shot at the DOE led African-American oversight staff came in my final week. ETMC had received a three-month extension on the first three years of the contract. The DOE was turning the operation of their water treatment plant over to the city of Oak Ridge. Due to complications in the negotiations for the transition between the two, we could not layoff the water treatment plant operators that were on our payroll. I had a major concern. The city of Oak Ridge had determined they were unwilling to pay the operators the union wages they were receiving under our contract with DOE. My fear was that the operators would bail for other jobs before the transition could be finalized. I negotiated a special incentive package at double their severance pay entitlement with the DOE and the union representing the operators if they remained for the duration. All the operators stayed except one. She had already accepted a job with the Knoxville, Tennessee utility.

I finally received a call from Barbara Jackson, another African-American who had taken Marlena Clark's position. She told me that Oak Ridge City and DOE had reached an agreement and I could now give the water treatment plant operators their thirty-day notice. I asked her to submit this request in writing, for the record. She then told me there were no plans to provide a written request. My response was that without something in writing, I did not feel comfortable giving the notice and I would not carry out her request until I received written notification from DOE authorizing me to layoff the workers. She said she was ordering me to carry out her request. After a few minutes of this back and forth discussion, I told her that I had a resolution to the situation. After we hung up, I would send her an e-mail confirming her request that I immediately give notice to the water plant operators. I would also send copies of the e-mail throughout her chain of command. She frantically begged me not to do that. I told her the e-mail was coming and at that point I would proceed to give the operators notice. I never heard from her again. How insecure can a person be in an oversight role?

As expected, one of DOE's conditions for the contract renewal was that I be replaced as project manager. When Deathridge shared DOE's expectation that I be replaced, I told him to do what was best for ETMC. It was his responsibility to act in the best interest of the other employees who were a part of the project and workers at the home office. I told him that I was a big guy and could take care of myself. When my contract was not renewed, as expected, I was terminated. I left knowing that I did everything I needed to do to look out for the welfare of the people who worked for me and ETMC as a whole. The things I did were necessary and resulted in ETMC ultimately receiving the recognition it deserved for our performance.

Despite not having my contract renewed, I departed ETMC on good terms with Deathridge. We maintained an excellent working relationship during my tenure. We worked the "good guy, bad guy" roles to perfection. He was very fair in his dealings with me and I was compensated well through his internal bonus structure. I gained a lot of respect for Mark's business acumen and how he successfully managed the finances of his company. He could teach a lot of other minority business owners some valuable lessons.

Reflecting on those years, the entire process was a labor of love. Jim Hall, DOE Oak Ridge Operations Manager, made a remark before our employees that we were an outstanding contractor. He went on to say that we were probably the only outstanding contractor on the DOE reservation. The employees really enjoyed working and as promised, we actually had fun. I only had three grievances filed by the unions during the entirety of my three years there, and they were all resolved at my desk. It was a matter of me explaining to the union's satisfaction why I made the decision in question. I would then hand the grievance form back to the union representatives and watched them tear it up. The project was virtually injury free as well.

Regarding having fun, Sam Crass, our project engineering manager, had a list of everyone's birthday date and had given the local bakery the list in advance. He would go by the bakery and pick up a birthday cake for every employee and I would present it to them on his behalf. There were also the occasional pranks that were a part of our comradery. The wife of our employee, Brad Starkey, sold Mary Kay products and he would bring the orders placed by the women to the job site. Brad drove a very manly pick-up truck to work and it had a camper on the back for transporting his hunting dogs. Crass and Bill Scott, the construction manager, had a pink magnetic sign made up that read: "See Me for Mary Kay Products", and placed it on the passenger side door. Brad did not understand for the life of himself why all of the women were honking their horns at him. It all came together when he finally found the sign after returning home from jogging one evening.

The supervisors would occasionally become victims of the fun as well. Boyd Kitts, vehicle maintenance supervisor, met with his men to prepare for their annual Christmas breakfast at the shop. During the winter months, ETMC was responsible for snow removal. It required long hours and sometimes the men would not be able to go home. As a result, the shop had a full kitchen to prepare meals during these exercises. In the meeting, Kitts unilaterally proclaimed that there would not be any sausage gravy at that year's breakfast. When the meeting was over, they asked Kitts if he had invited me to the breakfast. He said, no, and that he would drive up to my office and extend the invitation in person.

While he was making his way to my office, I received a phone call from the shop. They shared the story about the sausage gravy and asked that I request that it be on the menu.

Kitts made his way to my office and extended the invitation. I gladly accepted and told him I was looking forward to having some more of that sausage gravy they had last year. Kitts left and stopped in the office next door to call the shop to inform them to add the ingredients for the sausage gravy to the grocery list.

On the day of the breakfast, everything was in order. I went through the line and got everything on my plate, except the sausage gravy. Kitts had been observing me. When I passed on the sausage gravy, he blurted out: "I thought that you liked sausage and gravy." The entire kitchen broke out into laughter. Kitts realized that his men had gotten over on him.

Crass and Scott were two of the best hires I made after ETMC was awarded the contract. DOE ended up getting the best of all worlds. I later learned that both were on the competing small business team for the DOE proposal that ETMC won and their team finished second to our bid. These hires were not planned. I had met Crass at the American Water Works Association's annual meeting, which was held in Toronto, Canada. Crass was a civil engineer by background and had worked at the DOE water plant under a previous contractor, Rust Engineering. Johnson Controls Federal Systems had succeeded Rust as the contractor of choice. I was introduced to Crass by Dan Kearney, the DOE technical contracting officer for the maintenance contract. We went out to dinner together while in Canada.

Six months into the contract, Dennis Lund, who had an environmental engineering background, decided that the work on the project was not as appealing as he'd hoped. He initially felt that the water plant processing operation would present more of an environmental challenge. He resigned and it opened the door for another divine intervention.

Having met Crass in Canada, I was aware that he was working for a company based in Atlanta, while he maintained a family home in Oliver Springs, Tennessee, which is a rock's throw from Oak Ridge. I got in touch with Crass and asked if he would entertain the idea of returning to Oak Ridge and work as the project engineer on the ETMC contract. The prospect of getting back home and working in a familiar environment was very appealing. I invited him up to discuss my proposal and the scope of work that would make up his job description.

On the day we were scheduled to meet, Crass arrived at around noon for his interview. Realizing the time, I suggested we begin the interview process over lunch. I selected the Oak Ridge Applebee's restaurant. As we entered Applebee's, Crass spotted an old friend sitting with some other gentlemen and he introduced them to me. One of the men was Bill Scott. Crass was not aware that I had previously set up an interview with Scott for another position on the ETMC project. I had never met Scott and found it odd that we would meet under these circumstances.

As a matter of courtesy, I let Dan Kearney know of my plans to hire Crass. He said he would like to run it by his boss, George Benedict, the DOE Assistant Manager for Construction. With DOE's endorsement, I offered and Crass accepted.

Scott was another challenge for me. Deathridge and I were looking to bring on a person with a strong construction management background to help market and expand opportunities on other contracts that were coming up for bid under the DOE umbrella. Scott was a former executive with the DOE Oak Ridge Operations and had worked under Benedict. He left after a dispute with the DOE top leadership over what for him was a matter of principle. He explained the circumstances surrounding his leaving DOE and shared that he felt it was in the best interest of ETMC for Deathridge to vet him with the current DOE leadership before the process could move forward. Deathridge did follow up on his suggestion and was advised that we should not hire Scott for political reasons. Deathridge made me aware of the decision and I informed him I would get back with Scott. I asked Scott to have dinner with me. Scott later told me that after he hung up, he told his wife I had bad news for him; however, he appreciated that I was willing to tell him face to face. Of course, Scott was correct in his assessment of the situation. I closed our meeting by telling him that this may not be over and that potentially working for ETMC was not out of the question.

Several months later, God decided to intervene again. Dan Kearney called Crass and me to his office for a meeting. He said that based on a safety study, DOE was advised that there were potential risks associated with the water plant's five million gallon water storage tank. The study revealed that in the event of an earthquake, the tank could be compromised and the water coming off the hill could result in fatalities on the main road leading into the DOE Y-12 complex. DOE was awarded a special $1.5 million of additional funding to be added to the existing ETMC contract. It would be our responsibility to seek bids for a subcontractor with expertise in this area to perform the work. I told Kearney that since this was not in our original scope of work, it would be necessary to hire a construction manager for the project. He agreed.

I immediately called Bill Scott to ask him to go out to dinner with me and I offered him the job right on the spot. He accepted and was added to our team. To heck with this vetting stuff. I will hire a person with integrity any day. I did not inform the DOE regarding this decision on Scott until he reported to work.

This turned out to be one of my better decisions. Kearney had presented us the drawings from a local architectural engineering firm for the purpose of establishing the Request for Proposal. The successful bidder was a firm based in Pennsylvania. Upon reviewing the DOE drawings in greater detail, the firm's engineering staff discovered that the specs represented by the drawings would not accomplish the end result of preventing a failure of the five million gallon tank. The calculations were off. Scott reviewed their concerns and was in agreement that DOE needed to get back with the design firm and submit revised drawing which would resolve the issues.

ETMC now had a huge problem. We had an awarded contract with a limited budget of $1.5 million; however, the contractor was unable to begin work which could lead to penalties that we would have to pay for causing a delay in the start-up.

Scott had previously established a good relationship with the owners of the subcontracting company. We were relieved when they informed Scott that they had another job in Nevada. The owners told Scott they would fulfill their contract there and come back to our job at a later date, when the design issues were resolved. Scott reported to me that they also indicated they would not expect any penalty payments.

When all the issues were resolved, Scott and the subcontractor eventually brought the project in $100,000 under budget. God is good!

I left ETMC in 2000. Our management team of Scott, Crass, and I still meet quarterly and are joined by Dan Kearney, the former project DOE technical contracting officer. Early in the contract, he took another assignment and moved to Germany and was replaced by George Herron. I have even picked up a new friend in Bobby Scott, who was affiliated with these guys on the project under a previous contractor.

My management style can be attributed to my working for Colonel Duggins during my tour in the Republic of Vietnam. We had a great advisory team there, and I had a great contracting team in Oak Ridge.

Store front of Sights & Sounds Video

ACT I Movie Rentals. My second store following the closure of Sight & Sounds

Project Manager Hank Sauer and me at TRESP's
Oak Ridge, Tennessee headquarters

ETMC receives Award of Excellence. Pictured with water plant operators and
maintenance staff. President Mark Deathridge accepts the award

My Reunion with Colonel Duggins

As I continue to connect the dots identifying God's interventions in my life, I must share the coincidences surrounding my reunion with retired Col. Frank Duggins, Jr. The colonel had more influence over the man that I became than anyone outside of Mom. He came into my life when I was eighteen, probably the most impressionable period of my maturation into manhood. I wish every young African-American male could experience the mentoring I received from Colonel Duggins.

Having graduated from college and been successful as a business executive, I found the need to contact him. We had not been in communication since he left his assignment at the West Point Preparatory Academy, probably twenty-five years or longer.

Not having a clue as to where to start my search, it dawned on me that he was a graduate of the U.S. Army Military Academy at West Point. I called their alumni office in hopes they would have a record of him and a current address. The lady I spoke with placed me on hold and came back with a current address in Marshall, Missouri. I immediately called long distance directory assistance and was able to get his home telephone number.

I excitedly called and provided him with an update on my career, my family, and even discussed former Advisory Team #57 members, as I had continued to keep in touch with a number of them. He brought me up to date on his family and discussed some of the officers who were close to me in Vietnam.

I followed up this telephone reunion with an annual call to him every Christmas Day. As fate would have it, my oldest daughter, Tara, was graduating from the University of Tennessee with a degree in industrial engineering. She had accepted a job with Hallmark Cards, Inc., which is headquartered in Kansas City, Missouri. Karen, her mom, and I drove to Missouri with Tara to assist her in finding housing. I took the opportunity to surprise Colonel Duggins during our visit.

Marshall was a little over an hour's drive from Kansas City. The colonel's wife conspired with me in pulling off the surprise. One of the things I was most excited about was that my family had an opportunity to meet the man who was such an integral part of my life.

Once my daughter got settled into her job, I flew out to visit her. I rented a car and drove to Marshall to meet up with the colonel again. We were able to spend an entire day together reminiscing. He had two daughters, and I had three girls. His wife told me it was good for him to have me around for guy talk.

That day was the last time I saw Duggins. I still made my annual Christmas Day calls. His daughters and their families were generally present and one of them would invariably answer before handing the phone to him for our conversation.

One evening in June 2006, he was on my mind and I decided to deviate from tradition and call. I did not get an answer; however, I left a message on his answering machine.

Two weeks later I received a call from his daughter, Molly. She was at his house, decided to listen to his messages and saw that I had called. She told me her father had passed three weeks earlier. It was a sad day for me. I was able to tell her how much I thought of her dad. She told me how proud he was of me and how much he appreciated and looked forward to my calls every year. I told her I had some mementoes that I would like to share with the family. We decided that on my next trip to visit Tara, I would get together with her and older sister, Kathleen. She gave me her contact information to coordinate the luncheon we were planning.

I did not return to the Kansas City area until October of that year. Kathleen made the twenty minute drive from Lawrence, Kansas and Molly traveled from her home in the St. Louis, Missouri, area. It was an emotional luncheon. I gave them pictures of their father greeting comedienne Martha Raye when she landed to visit our team. I included an article on how Raye refused to take an evacuation helicopter and used her nursing skills to assist wounded soldiers when another unit she was visiting was attacked. There was also a picture taken with Hugh O'Brien, the actor who played Wyatt Earp in the television show.

Finally, there was a copy of the song, *The Song of Vinh Binh: Hello Charlie,* that three artillery officers had written as a tribute to Duggins (Charlie was a nickname for the Viet Cong). Majors Hal Luck, Don DeVilbiss, and Arch Bassham had stored enough ammunition to have a special barrage of artillery to rain down on Viet Cong strongholds on the evening of July 4, 1966.

The officers wrote the lyrics on a napkin in a bar and sung the song to the tune of *Hello Dolly*. VC in the phonetic alphabet is "Victor Charlie."

The Song of Vinh Binh "Hello Charlie"

Oh hello Charlie, say! Hello Charlie
Hope you enjoy our fireworks show tonight.
I hear the guns banging,
And I'll bet you're draggin'
Your 'ole' rear out to the nearest foxhole.
It's Independence Day, Charlie
You've gone the wrong way, Charlie
Don't you know that you will never, ever win?
So, dig a little deeper Charlie,
Here comes another volley,
Charlie will never be the same again.

One of the most meaningful things I brought to this luncheon meeting was information the family was missing. They told me their mom had passed before their dad, and they said she was disappointed she never became a general's wife. That disappointment was also felt by the men who served under him.

Duggins' graduation from West Point in 1952 came during the middle of the Korean War. He, along with his classmates, were called to serve in this conflict. Surviving, Duggins received assignments that lead to his becoming a lieutenant colonel at the age of 36–which was considered a young age for that rank.

During the luncheon, I was able to share with his family the decision he made that derailed his career. While with Advisory Team #57, our observer pilot (Shotgun 15) spotted a Chinese flagged trawler unloading weapons and ammunition at one of the Viet Cong strong-holds on the Son Co Hoau River. This was during a ceasefire period and protocol required that neither side could advance their positions. Duggins sent a request up the chain of command for permission to attack the trawler. After receiving a decision, our team was told to stand-down. Duggins passed the order on to Shotgun 15 and advised him to return to base.

Several weeks later, after the ceasefire was over, either this same Chinese flagged trawler (or one similar) was spotted by Shotgun 15 doing the same thing. He radioed to base and asked to speak to Duggins. When Duggins learned of the situation, he turned and asked someone to call an artillery officer to the radio room. With the artillery officer present, the colonel asked Shotgun 15 for the coordinates of the trawler's location. A short time later, Duggins radioed Shotgun 15 to inform him to stand by and that artillery was on its way. Within a few minutes, Shotgun 15 communicated that the trawler had received a direct hit, and he was observing several secondary explosions from the munitions on board. Duggins's position was that those arms and munitions were going to be used to shoot at his team and to him that was an unacceptable condition. After all, we were fighting a war.

Apparently the chain of command did not appreciate his actions. Duggins was called to a meeting at MACV Headquarters in Saigon to discuss his decision. He reiterated that those weapons were going to be used against the men that served under him, and as their commander there was no way he was going to let that happen. The colonel stood his ground. "Conviction and comfort don't live on the same block."

Their displeasure with him was reflected in his performance evaluation. This ultimately prevented him from getting the types of assignments that would keep him on track to become a general. General Frank H. Duggins, Jr. has a great ring to it; however, I will take my courageous and principled Colonel Duggins any day.

I felt that God used me to bring comfort to a family who needed an answer to a question that was long overdue for them. They now had a greater appreciation for the admiration and respect Duggins achieved from those who had the honor to serve under his command, and now they also know why.

There's another irony associated with my relationship with Duggins and his family. My youngest daughter, Ashley, graduated from the University of Tennessee with an electrical engineering degree. She also accepted a job with Hallmark and was assigned to their processing plant in Lawrence, Kansas and established a residence there. Lawrence is the home to the University of Kansas where the husband of Duggins's daughter, Kathleen, was on the faculty. What are the chances of Colonel Duggins and James Bussell both having daughters living in Lawrence, Kansas at the same time?

There will always be a connection between Molly, Kathleen, and me. The joy of reminiscing about the colonel will always be special.

Colonel Duggins greets comedienne Martha Raye on her visit to Advisory Team #57 (1966)

My reunion with Retired Colonel Frank H. Duggins, Jr. at his home in Marshall, Missouri (2000)

DEPARTMENT OF THE ARMY

U. S. MILITARY ACADEMY PREPARATORY SCHOOL

FORT BELVOIR, VIRGINIA 22060

9 December 1966

MAPS

SP5 James B. Bussell
RA 14 856 134
Advisory Team 57
APO San Francisco 96314

Dear Bus,

    Heard from Major Wells about the Cang Long episode -
a shame. What happened to Captain Higgins and Maj Ky?
I'm enclosing a letter I sent to Maj (L/C Chandler - which may
not have reached him prior to departure. If you can check
on any of the items I would appreciate it.

    This is a fine assignment and I would like to see you
apply for school here. I believe you can make it through
West Point - if you want to! (and aren't _too_ old). I'm
enclosing a copy of our AR on what to do. I'm also
inclosing a letter to Col Tahn which I wish you would give
to him.

    Appreciated your letter - keep me informed - keep up
the good work - and give my very best to all the team,
Col B, Sgts Dinh and Hoi, Chef Lin, Yap, Yan, MUI'!!.
Dai Ui Mui, Dan, Bruce, John - and all for a Merry Christmas
and a better New Year
        WANG HO VIET NAM.

FRANK H. DUGGINS, JR.
LTC, Inf.
Commandant

P.S. Did anyone ever submit the P.C. for
      an award - US type?

**LTC Duggins letter inviting me to apply for enrollment at the West
Point Preparatory School where he became Commandant after leaving
Advisory Team #57**

Luncheon with Colonel Duggins's daughters Molly Crews (center)
and Kathleen Smith.

Going Postal—Laughter Is the Best Medicine

E arlier I cited Jerimiah 29:11 regarding God's plan for me. There is no greater evidence than what happened to me near the end of my work career. One of the downsides to changing jobs, going into business for yourself, and working in small firms is there are very few opportunities to build a retirement pension. I was in my late fifties and had a small pension I started receiving from the TVA retirement system when I turned fifty-five. My wife was working full time with the Knox County Board of Education and was able to provide the family with health and dental insurance through her employer.

I was now between jobs for the umpteenth time. I had recently resigned from Pioneer Builders where I was serving as the project manager of Runway-Visual-Range installation contract for the Federal Aviation Administration at Knoxville's McGhee-Tyson Airport. Pioneer Builders was a small, struggling minority-owned company which had won the contract with FAA as a special Small Business Administration Section 8(a) set-a-side. I resigned when Phase I, the major portion of the contract, was completed. Phase II amounted to tearing down old structures that were no longer necessary after being replaced by the RVR installation. The owner of the company refused to require his subcontractor to complete work in a timely manner that was critical to our schedule. His lack of action resulted in Pioneer Builders missing the FAA contractual completion deadline by two weeks. He was seemly intimidated by the owner of the subcontractor firm and forbade me from dealing with him for fear I would run him off. He did not understand we had the leverage, in fact, this particular subcontractor had performance payments due from Pioneer Builders totaling approximately $200,000. My attitude was we would not make any progress payments until his key people showed up and performed the work on a timely basis. The Pioneer Builder's owner would not budge.

Although I was expected to manage Phase II, I resigned to allow the owner to find someone more compatible to his management style. The word failure was not a part of my vocabulary, and I was disappointed that a project I managed did not meet the FAA contractual deadline. My resignation was effective in October 2000.

As November approached, I immediately began looking for a job to tide me over until the next opportunity. My inclination, with the Christmas season approaching, was to go to United Parcel Service to see when their seasonal hiring would begin. I interviewed with their local human resources representative who informed me they were in fact hiring; however, the jobs consisted of working on a truck with a regular driver with a five hours per day limit. Divine intervention happened to me again. Recognizing that I was interesting in a 40-hour week position, she referred me to the United States Postal Service. She knew they were hiring full-time workers for the Christmas season.

I immediately followed-up with the USPS and completed the required drug screening. I was hired two days later as a casual mail handler at the Knoxville Processing and Distribution Center Plant. The plant had four labor categories: mail processing clerks, mail handlers, electronic technicians, and custodial. The pay was $12 an hour with no benefits. Due to union contractual agreements, the casuals were limited to forty-hours per week. The plant could work us up to twelve hours a day without paying overtime after 8 hours, as was the case for the union employees. Some weeks we only worked three and half days because we would be sent home when we hit the forty-hour maximum.

As it turned out, the good performers were maintained after the holiday season. The maximum tenure in a craft for a casual employee was six months; however the game was after six months they would lay you off for three days and bring you back in another craft as a casual. I did this for about eighteen months. Finally, the postal service staffing needs reached a level where they scheduled their prerequisite examination to allow people to apply for part-time flex positions. This would give the successful candidates access to the complete benefits package to include health insurance, paid vacation, sick leave and other benefits. There were no limits to the number of hours you were allowed to work; however, they only guaranteed thirty-two hours per week. Overtime pay was authorized for all hours over forty in a week at time-and-a-half.

I passed the exam with a composite score of ninety-two for the clerical portion and ninety-six for the mail handler portion. This practically placed me at the top of the list for the next round of hiring, and I ended up taking the first opportunity that came along. Although I scored higher on the mail handler portion, the first offer was a clerical position at the South Knoxville Post Office as a window clerk.

This is where the fun began. I reached back to my own personal experience of dealing with seemly inattentive and sometimes rude window clerks. My approach would be customer driven, presenting a good image to the public. I would have my shirts starched. This really impressed the some of the older women customers. I discovered a lot of the older customers came to the post office as a part of their weekly ritual. They would rarely buy a book of stamps, but would purchase enough to tide them over to justify another trip. I always tried to inject humor into my dealings with the customers and learn their names. The people in line seemed to appreciate the humor which made their wait more interesting.

In an effort to get me more hours, my postal manager would lend me out to other locations when these offices were experiencing personnel shortages. On one occasion, I was sent to the Cedar Bluff Station, which was one of the busiest in the entire State of Tennessee, and noted for its long lines. On one particular day, a customer from France came in, accompanied by his American host, to ship belongings back to his native country. He had two large boxes. I placed the first one on the scale and it reflected a cost of over a $150.00 to send it by air. He asked if I had anything cheaper. I reweighed the package and determined that it would cost about seventy-nine dollars to ship it by surface. He kept asking: "Is there something cheaper?" We went through the same scenario with the second package. It was obvious these two gentlemen were having fun with me. When I rang up the total, his final question was: "Are you sure that you have nothing cheaper?" My response, to the delight of the other customers who were standing in line was: "Well, yes. We have a pack mule out back, but you are going to have to feed it and teach it how to swim." The Frenchman paid his tab and bade me adieu.

My favorite story happened to another clerk at another station. It seemed that a little old lady, estimated to be in her eighties, came up to the window clerk and expressed that she had a problem with her mail delivery. She said she had not received mail in over four days. Her concern was there was not a day that went by where she did not at least get some junk mail.

The window clerk paged the station's delivery supervisor. After hearing the story, he told her he needed to go back to his office and check on it. He came back and proudly informed her that he had found the answer to the problem. He said the regular postman was in the hospital and that a substitute carrier was delivering mail to her neighborhood addresses. Digesting what the supervisor had just told her, she asked the supervisor: "Does this mean that should my carrier die, I will not get mail anymore?" Chalk one up for the sharp little old lady.

Back at the South Knoxville Post Office, I had a personal experience with an older white female customer who I later learned was a widow who played bridge in the afternoon with other neighborhood ladies. It was apparent that they drank something other than tea. She was in the back of the line when I heard a voice saying: "You need to cover up that bald head." Since I was the only bald window clerk, I decided to ignore her. Her reaction was to say: "You heard me." I just smiled and kept waiting on customers. Then I noticed she was passing up open windows and waiting for me. All the while she continued to attempt to engage me in conversation. The other customers were having a ball with this. When she got to my window, she asked me if I was married. I told her, yes. She then asked if I wanted a girlfriend on the side. I told her I would check with my wife to see if it was OK and get back with her. As she was leaving, she asked for my phone number. I told her it was in the telephone book. She said OK, James, but I don't have your last name. I told her that it was in the book, too.

In 2008, the Knoxville Processing and Distribution Center announced a series of full-time regular openings for which existing PTF's could apply. I ended up with a processing clerk position on a 1:30 p.m. to 10:00 p.m. shift. This is when I realized the postal service management was the most dysfunctional group of supervisors in the world.

I had experience working in and around a lot of federal agencies and had seen a lot of bureaucracies. Nothing tops the USPS. There were one or two exceptions; however, by and large most were just incompetent, indifferent and seemly not at all concerned about customer service. Judging by some of the directives we received from the upper echelons in the chain of command, this incompetence went beyond the local plant level. With regard to customer service, I had an experience while at the South Knoxville Station that demonstrates how managers were not committed to customer service. Following a stamp rate increase, the USPS issued two-cent stamps to cover the increase for customers who had stamps remaining from the previously priced stamps. This was before the development of the "forever stamp". Our station manager decided not to issue the stamps to the window clerks to sell to the affected customers. His reasoning was that he was scheduled to do a stamp inventory in a few days, and by not opening the packets of two-cent stamps, it would make his count easier. Therefore, we had to inconvenience our customers by requiring them to make an extra trip to another station to get their two-cent stamps. I attempted to convince the station manager, if he would let us sell the stamps, he would not have to count them at all, but to no avail.

At one time, I had a goal of using my management experience to eventually apply for the USPS management training program. It did not take me long to realize that I would not be happy as a manager there. I decided to continue my career on the floor as a mail processing clerk. I could write a book to cover my experience at the mail processing plant, with the other option of going on *Comedy Central* and tell these real life stories.

At the processing plant, the work did not require a lot of supervision. I am convinced the employees could efficiently handle the mail without having a supervisor on the floor at all. Many of the employees have been there long term and know the process like the backs of their hands. The process was pretty much straight forward. Trucks back up to the docks with incoming mail. The mail handlers unload the trucks, breakdown the mail, and transport the containers to the appropriate processing section of the plant. The clerks would process the mail for dispatching to the stations. The mail handlers would pick the mail up at the processing sections and take it to the dock for dispatch to the area post offices. Not rocket science!

Supervisors were responsible for making out the daily schedules for their respective subordinates. I am convinced that if the supervisors made out the schedule and went to their office for the balance of the shift, the mail would be processed in a timely fashion.

As with all organizations, there were some lazy individuals who were not going to perform and there was not a lot management could do about it. The unions had objected to including performance standards in the contracts. By and large the rank and file postal employees get a bad rap, with a great majority of them wanting to get the mail out in a timely fashion. They recognize that it is the customer who is paying their salaries and deserves good service. It was management that was indifferent and, in most cases, responsible for delaying the mail.

My best example of this was on a shift with approximately forty-five clerks, there would always be one or two stragglers who would exceed the five minute grace period for clocking in for the start of the shift. The grace period was designed so that people who were on time would not be penalized if there was a lot of traffic at the clock. When the employee missed the grace period, the supervisor was required to go into the computer software and adjust the time manually. The supervisors became frustrated with the process and decided that at the end of the day's shift, we were all to drop our time cards into a locked box. They renovated an office at the employee entrance and put a system in place where the cards would be placed in slots for us to retrieve when we came to work the next day. A supervisor manned the office and after the five minute grace period, anyone coming to work late would not have access to their time card. (The cards were on a board that rotated after the grace period.) The employee would then have to get the supervisor manning the office to have their time manually adjusted. At this point they could retrieve their card. A stroke of genius on their part? Not really. On the first day of implementing the new system, someone forgot to leave the key to the box where we had deposited our time cards at the end of the previous shift. No one had access to their time card and none of us could clock in for our shift. Now the supervisor had to manually process forty-five clerks instead of the customary two or three. This innovative concept on the part of supervision lasted about a week. The employees did not trust the system and stopped placing their cards in the box.

Another favorite story at the plant was the utilization of regular clerks to become what was referred as 204(b)s. This designation was a reference to a provision in the union contract that management could select volunteer clerks to help supervise on the floor. They would receive additional compensation over and beyond their normal hourly rate. In most cases the only people who wanted to be 204(b)s were the laziest and the least productive ones on the shift. One such employee was accepted into the 204(b) program and was assigned to supervise his former crew. When he arrived to check on their performance, he discovered all of them sitting at their respective work stations reading a magazine. They ignored his order to go to work and he ended up paging one of the regular supervisors. When the regular supervisor arrived, he asked the crew: "What are you doing?" Their response was: "The same thing your 204(b) did when he worked over here with us."

A new supervisor took over our section. I had a unique problem with her. I would show up for work every day. I would be standing at the clock, along with my co-workers, for her daily instructions prior to posting the assignments for our shift. The problem was she would forget to place me on the schedule. It didn't matter to me since I was on the clock and was getting paid.

I would go over and remind her she did not place me on schedule, and she would apologize and give me an assignment. This did not just happen one or two times. She apparently had a mental block that prevented her from listing me or had an outdated shift roster. After the third time, I stopped reminding her and would be on my own for the shift. I would identify areas where help was needed and support the shift in that way, taking my own initiative to be productive. The exception came during March Madness of the NCAA Basketball Tournament. I decided that, since my supervisor did not appreciate my efforts, I would head to the break room and watch basketball. I knew that at some point during the shift someone would turn me in to her.

It was some time after the first scheduled employee break, which came two hours from the beginning of the shift, that she located me in the break room, all alone, watching basketball. She immediately told me how disappointed she was with me and indicated that she no longer felt bad about leaving me off the schedule. She told me that the next time she left me off the schedule I was to tell her immediately.

My response was that USPS was not paying me to tell her how to do her job. She said it was a direct order. I told her if she appreciated my productivity, she would put me on the schedule. As for the direct order, I would ignore it. I said it would be a lot easier for me to explain why I was in the break room than for her to explain why I was there. I was never left off the schedule again.

My favorite supervisors at the plant were Linda Flynn and Carl Ursery. Both knew their jobs and treated everyone fairly. They also knew how to make assignments and did not bother the productive workers on the shift. Ursery was African-American and was deservingly promoted to the next level of Manager for Distribution Operations.

Flynn and I had an amusing experience. One morning the home phone rang with caller-ID indicating a postal service number. It was Flynn calling to ask if I would be available to come to work two hours early, to get a head-start on the volume of mail waiting for our shift at the plant. I had pushed the button on our speaker phone and my wife was in ear shot and privy to the conversation. I informed Flynn that I would be there and she said, "Okay, thanks sweetie." Karen asked: "Did she just call you sweetie?" I jokingly responded: "You should hear what she calls me at work when I'm rubbing her back." End of discussion. When I arrived at work, I shared the conversation that my wife and I had after she hung up. We still laugh about that phone call today.

The custodian knows best. Charlie was the custodian on our shift. Following an overnight snow fall, either the plant manager or the postmaster noticed the sidewalks to the customer service area had not been salted and cleared. When he came back to the processing section of the plant, he realized the employee entrance had not been salted and cleared either. He immediately summoned Charlie and inquired as to why the snow was not salted around the critical areas of the plant. Charlie explained to him that OSHA required a plant of our size to have X number of bags of salt on hand at all times, but he only had one bag of salt for the entire facility. He then asked the most important question of the day: "Where do you want me to put it?" Needless to say, the maintenance supervisor did not have a good day.

God placed me with the USPS to allow me to build up a retirement. The postal service, in an effort to keep their employment numbers down, relied heavily on overtime for its workers. Employees had the option each quarter to sign-up for the overtime list. Employees who opted out could not be forced to work overtime unless management called for mandatory overtime during critical manpower shortages. Management would have to require the entire shift to stay over under these circumstances. As a processing clerk, the job was not that difficult. I had a wonderful partner in Carolyn Dix. She had been a year ahead of me in high school, and we both possessed the same work ethic. We were the envy of the plant in that we had fun on the job. She and I both signed up for the overtime list. That made the overtime fun and the time would pass by quickly, whether we were working two hours or four hours overtime, which was paid at time-and-a-half for all hours over eight. Premium overtime of double-time would be paid for all hours over ten. The overtime list also gave us the option of working on our scheduled days off. In this case, we would receive time and a half for the shift and double time after eight hours.

I made myself available for each of these options. My goal was to live on my base salary and bank my overtime into the Thrift Savings Plan, the federal government's version of a 401(k) plan. During this time, banks were only paying 1 percent or less on savings. By placing funds in the TSP, I received a guarantee of 4 percent dividend from the fund; in addition, the postal service provided for a matching contribution of up to five percent.

Being over fifty-five years old, I was able to take advantage of the U.S. Internal Revenue Service's retirement catch-up provision. This allowed those of us who qualified to put in as much as $5,000 above the allowable contribution, which would be exempted from payroll taxes until the money is withdrawn during retirement.

In October 2012 at age 66, I was eligible to begin drawing my full Social Security benefits. Around this time, the postal service announced an early retirement incentive to encourage older workers to leave the company. Employees accepting the incentive would be terminated on January 31, 2013. The incentive was a payment of $15,000 to be paid in two installments. The first payment of $10,000.00 paid at retirement. The $5,000.00 balance to be paid in May 2014. I decided to accept the incentive. My last day of work was January 25, 2013.

God continued his plan for me by providing financial stability for retirement. I did not have a solid retirement savings when I began working for the USPS. Once I reached my five year milestone, I was eligible to continue paying and receiving family health insurance benefits after retirement. Knowing that I could provide a better coverage at retirement, my wife was able to retire early from her job with the school system based on incentives they had offered to their employees for a similar reason.

My Field of Dreams

As in the 1989 movie *Field of Dreams,* a fantasy film about baseball, my dream of playing major league baseball was fulfilled in the form of the 2013 San Francisco Giants Baseball Fantasy Camp. A little history is in order to completely understand how God intervened again, as if it was His plan for me all along.

My ambition as a small child was to play professional baseball. In the early days in Lynch, Kentucky, I lived next door to a player for the Lynch Greys Semi-Pro baseball team. Jack Amos was a coal miner by occupation, but was also the catcher for the Greys. Weekends in the summer were filled with games at the local baseball park, as other semi-pro teams would come to town to take on the Lynch Greys, including teams from our family's roots in Knoxville.

There were also four little league teams in Lynch. At nine years old, I played one year for the Lynch Cubs before moving to Knoxville. That was the end of my baseball experienced until about six years later. I was raised in rural Knox County, and there were not enough kids to field a little league baseball team in my age group. There was, however, a men's semi-pro team called the Bearden Tigers where my older cousin, Arthur, and all of his friends played. They were one of the most competitive teams in the Knoxville area. They played in a league with most of their games at Leslie Street Park in the Mechanicsville neighborhood. Bearden would host some local and out of town teams at the West High School baseball diamond.

At age 15, I tried out to be the batboy for the team. There was an older man that the neighbors called "Funnyboy," who would informally handle the chores. As far as I knew, the team did not have an official batboy. I took the initiative of showing up at the practices and helped team manager, John Ed Cornelius, unload the equipment and get set-up. Since many of the players had full-time jobs, it was understood that everyone could not make practice on time. Eventually, a full complement of players would be there before practice was over.

I would always take my glove and warm up some of the players who showed up late. As time went on, I would go out on the field and play a position that needed to be fielded due to the late arrival of a player. During infield practice, I would end up playing all of the positions and did the same thing in the outfield. Other players noticed that I was not afraid of the ball and had a strong throwing arm returning the balls back to the infield.

As we wrapped up the pre-season practices and Cornelius began issuing the uniforms, he gathered the team around and announced that I was not going to be the batboy. You could not imagine the disappointment I felt. I had committed myself all spring for that opportunity and now I was being told I did not make the grade. After hesitating for what seemed like an eternity, Cornelius handed me a uniform and informed me that the team felt I was good enough to be a player. At fifteen, I was playing semi-pro baseball for the Bearden Tigers. I was the team's utility player, meaning I was not a designated starter. I would substitute for any player missing for a game at any position except pitcher and catcher. I was a solid fielder and my throwing arm won the respect of the opposing teams after throwing players out at home plate from the outfield. Life didn't get better than that!

The thing I was most excited about was these teams and their leagues were sources for major league talent. Most of the major league teams had local scouts on their payroll. Many thought that our shortstop, Leonard Foxx, had the best potential. He was a solid hitter and fielder. Many felt he did not make the major leagues because, over the years, he developed a habit of throwing the ball with sort of underhanded and sidearm motion.

I had the opportunity to play against Harry Wilson, Sr., who in 1950, was one of the first African-American pitchers to be drafted by a major league team from the East Tennessee area. Harry was drafted by the Saint Louis Browns and went to spring training, which the club held in San Antonio, Texas. He unfortunately stepped in a drain in the outfield and broke his leg shagging fly balls. He returned to Knoxville to recover and for personal reasons, never returned. He remained a premier pitcher in our league for years and his love of the game never waned. After the Bearden Tigers disbanded, I had the honor of playing for him years later when he was the player-coach for the East Knoxville Cubs. It is important to note that at age forty-eight, Wilson pitched a no-hit game against players from the Roane State Community College baseball team in nearby Harriman, which played in our summer Stan Musial Semi-Pro League.

During my playing days with the East Knoxville Cubs, a Negro League Hall of Fame player, Eugene Williams, joined our team following his retirement. Gene was signed by the St. Louis Cardinals in 1953 and was traded to the Chicago White Sox organization. He was assigned to their AAA affiliate team until he was injured in 1956. He left the White Sox organization and joined the Negro League Memphis Red Sox. There he had the distinction of being a teammate of country music singer Charlie Pride. Gene also played for the Birmingham Black Barons.

At fifteen, I had a problem. The Bearden Tigers would travel some weekends throughout East Tennessee and southeastern Kentucky to play teams in these areas, but Mom would not allow me to travel with these men. In most cases, following the games they would end up at the local night clubs to socialize with the opposing teams. At the time most of these towns were located in dry counties, meaning that serving or possession of alcohol was illegal. Therefore, most of these night clubs were illegal and were subject to being raided if the club owners did not have "special arrangements" with the local sheriffs.

Up steps Doc Miller, one of the neighborhood alcoholics. On the morning of our out of town games, Miller would show up at our home sober and begin begging Mom to let me go with the team. He committed to be personally responsible for me. Mom reminded him that he drank and there was no way he could be responsible for her son. Miller was very persuasive and convinced Mom there was the potential we would not have enough players and explained my value as a utility player. He also promised her he would not be drinking on the trip. Mom agreed to let me go.

What she didn't know was that Doc would be drunk before the convoy of cars pulled out for the trip to the town where we would be playing. We did in fact end up in these nightspots. Out of respect for

Mom, I only drank cokes. What was interesting, is that I rode in the car that Miller was travelling in to allow me to make sure that he got home OK. His live-in-girlfriend always thanked me for seeing him to the door and helping place him on the couch to allow him to sleep it off.

This scenario played out throughout the summer. As much as I liked baseball, I also loved the attention I drew in my uniform. On weekends, when we had an afternoon or early evening game, I would put on my uniform first thing in the morning and walk around the neighborhood all day. In most cases, I would have my ball and glove, simply walking and pitching the ball in the air and catching it.

This ritual got me busted. Someone had noticed and complemented me to Mom regarding how well I would take care of Miller on these road trips. Miller's girlfriend had apparently told this neighbor she would not let Doc go on these trips unless James went, knowing I would at least make sure he got home OK.

Mom confronted me with this newly found information regarding the road trips and asked me was it true. I confessed that what she had heard was accurate. I thought surely this was the end of the road trips for me. Mom shocked me: "Go join your team." She sounded proud that her fifteen year old was man enough to take care of both Doc Miller and himself; however, Doc Miller walked into a buzz saw the next time he approached Mom regarding taking care of me on these road trips.

I had two summers with the Bearden Tigers. The summer I was approaching my eighteenth birthday, I enlisted in the U.S. Army. Believe it or not, having the experience with these older men taught me a lot of good life lessons. Most of them had dropped out of high school to caddy at Cherokee Country Club. Others worked as orderlies at the local hospitals, mostly cleaning up after patients and transporting them. These things were not on my list of career choices. There was a common denominator among these guys. Around the time they reached twenty-one, they would get drafted into the military. In many cases their lives had been coming together, either finally saving enough to buy the car they wanted or serious about a girlfriend they wanted to marry, when Uncle Sam came calling.

These observations played a big part in my decision to enlist in the Army at seventeen with my high school diploma in hand. I avoided becoming a domestic worker and satisfied my military obligation at the same time. The other consideration was making a career of the Army. That decision would come later.

I continued playing semi-pro baseball well into my forties. Like Harry Wilson, my love of the game never waned. From that little kid in Lynch, Kentucky in the early fifties, I became a big fan of Willie Mays and the New York Giants. I followed his career after he was discharged from the Army and immediately lead the Giants to a World Series victory over the Cleveland Indians in 1954. My loyalty followed Mays and the Giants in their transition to San Francisco, California.

After getting discharged from the Army, I would drive to Atlanta to catch the San Francisco Giants when they came to town to play the Braves in a weekend series. I would attend all three games. I knew all of Mays's stats and record breaking achievements. This would benefit me later.

Anticipating retirement in September 2012, I signed up for the San Francisco Giants Baseball Fantasy Camp, which was to be held at their spring training facility in Scottsdale, Arizona. This was at the top of my retirement bucket list.

My last day at the Post Office was January 25, 2013. The following Sunday, on January 27th, I boarded a plane to Scottsdale to spend a week playing baseball at the age of 66. What was most appealing regarding the camp were the eighteen former San Francisco Giants players, including Vida Blue, Shawn Estes, and Russ Ortiz from the modern era of Giant's baseball, who were there. These former players were paired up to serve as coaches for the sixteen teams, made up of the 102 players who had signed up for the camp.

During the reception on Sunday night, which served as an introduction of the former players and the camp participants, I was not as much interested in the modern players as I was in Mike McCormick and Jimmy Davenport. They were special to me because they had played with Willie Mays on the 1962 World Series team that lost to Mickey Mantle and the New York Yankees in seven games. I migrated to them and immediately enjoyed the pleasure of hearing their stories about their playing days in the 60s. I was pleasantly surprised following tryouts on Monday, when the coaches evaluated the players and drafted their respective teams. McCormick and Davenport had drafted me to be one of their players.

The bonus to all of this was the amount of time I had to spend with these two guys, going down memory lane. One evening following the draft, the itinerary called for the coaches to have dinner with their respective teams. I ended up sitting next to Davenport. While discussing Willie Mays, I brought up the game in Milwaukee where Willie had hit four home runs in a single game. I told Davenport that I remembered Mays was on deck to possibly hit five homeruns when the last out was made before Mays could get the opportunity. Davenport responded by saying: "I made that last out". I could have never envisioned that the little boy from Lynch, Kentucky, with his baseball uniform, would one day be wearing the uniform of his baseball hero almost 60 years later. How cool is that?

The only thing that can top the above experience was the opportunity to play basketball in an exhibition game with the now late Crown Prince of Basketball, Meadowlark Lemon of the Harlem Globetrotters. Growing up, Lemon was another one of my heroes. I had seen him play in person when the Globetrotters made appearances in Knoxville. Following his retirement from the Globetrotters, Lemon became an ordained minister. As a part of his ministry, he formed a traveling team called the Harlem All-Stars, made up of some former Globetrotters. Lemon and his team were invited to Knoxville as a fundraiser for a local church. The promoter knew that, at the age of 64, I was still actively playing basketball. He asked that I pull together a team to play the All-Stars and I ended up being the player/coach for the players who competed in the exhibition game.

One of the blessings that allowed me to play basketball and baseball well into my sixties was my conditioning regiment. I have always operated on the premise that our bodies were a gift from God. It has been proven that if you take care of your body, the body will take care of you.

Paraphrasing a quote by Friedrich Nietzsche that I adopted, states: "In every real man, there is a little boy who wants to come out and play."[15] That quote certainly applies to me. Over the years, I have had the privilege of playing very competitive basketball at the downtown YMCA three times a week with my longtime friends Jerry Foster and, before he moved to West Virginia, Dick Symons. There would normally be fifteen to twenty guys who would show up to play on Tuesday and Thursday afternoons and Saturday morning. Foster and I would show up thirty minutes before everyone else and play two or three one-on-one games to the score of twenty-one. As you can image, we were both in top condition. Occasionally, when Symons's business travels had called for a trip to the Southeast, he routed his flight itinerary for an overnight stay in Knoxville. Foster and I have arrived at the YMCA at 5 p.m. on a number of occasions to find Dick standing at the front desk waiting to play basketball. This proves how structured our routine was. On one occasion, we were all downstairs in the locker room following the two hours of basketball when I was paged to come to the front desk for a phone call. Symons immediately commented to the other guys regarding how henpecked I was and said my wife knew where I was at all times. When I picked up the phone, I heard Symons' wife, Cindy, on the line. She had called my home asking for him. Karen had told her that if he was in Knoxville, he was probably with me at the downtown YMCA and she gave Cindy the number. I confirmed his presence and told her I would gladly go downstairs and get him. I had a huge grin on my face when I greeted Symons with the news that his wife in Ohio—where they had moved by this time—was on the phone and wanted to speak to him. I then said that at least my wife keeps up with me here in town.

What an overall experience! My dream of playing professional sports, whether baseball or basketball, never became a reality; however, God seemed to recognize my desire and in His own way rewarded me with a new and different experience when it came to sports. In the final analysis, I was able to have the best of all worlds—a successful professional career in business and the enjoyment of playing the sports that I loved as a hobby.

My first baseball uniform at age 5

With nephew Barry Bussell in Bearden Tigers baseball uniform at age 15 (1961)

San Francisco Giants Fantasy Camp locker at Scottsdale, Arizona Stadium (Giants Spring Training Facility). Wearing uniform and number 24 for my hero Willie Mays. Note: Uniform includes the SF Giants 2012 World Championship patch the Giants wore during the 2013 regular season. (2013)

Getting a hit during Fantasy Camp
Camp Photographer: Andy S. Kuno

Clubhouse photo from left to right: Cy Young Award Winner and American League
MVP Vida Blue, Jimmy Davenport, James Bussell and
Cy Young Award Winner Mike McCormick

Pictured with former San Francisco Giants Player who served as coaches
during the Fantasy Camp
Camp Photographer: Andy S. Kuno

My Fantasy baseball team with coaches Davenport (left) and
McCormick (right). I am in the center of the last row.
Camp Photographer: Andy S. Kuno

Playing against the Clown Prince of Basketball and retired member of the World
Famous Harlem Globetrotters Meadowlark Lemon. I am number 12. (2010)

My Family
From Left (Eric and Tara Boldridge w/daughters Jalyn and Nia; Derick and Ashley
Aye w/son Damien and daughter Brooklyn; Daughter Stacey Bussell
and Karen Bussell

Epilogue

When I began the process of putting thoughts to paper for this book, I did not realize the enormous number of anomalies that are associated with divine intervention in my life. What is amazing is that these anomalies are intertwined like a web of dots. It is clear to me that these seventy years of my life were scripted by God from the very beginning. He certainly demonstrated His faith in me long before I knew Him and the impact of His awesome power over the universe. He gave me great parents who understood that God is the foundation of everything good, and our family continues to be blessed today for the spiritual nurturing we received.

The only logic to account for the many events that shaped my life is God's guiding hands. The most significant part of this journey was dealing with adversaries and not becoming bitter in the process. In many cases, I sought out the best in these individuals and the rewards were astounding. This, of course, did not work in all cases. There were some who had character flaws, which I chose to accept and recognize that they were ones with the issues, not me.

Finally, my employment history throughout this book illustrates how my life has been guided by principles, integrity and an unwillingness to compromise my dignity in the process. On many occasions, opportunities for me have come from unexpected sources and demonstrates that God does things based on His schedule for us... not our own. This is by far the greatest lesson that I have learned about a life with God.

I do not think anyone can deny the scripture in Jerimiah 29:11 and how it has been applied to my life. Thanks for taking this journey with me. I will close with a quote from Romans 15:13: **May the God of hope fill you with all joy and peace as you trust in Him, so that you may overflow with hope by the power of the Holy Spirit." (NIV)**

Endnotes

1   National Center for Educational Statistics (NCES) is the primary federal entity for collecting and analyzing data related to education. Source: (nces.ed.gov/)

2   Center for Disease Control National Center for Health Statistics. National Vital Statistics Report Volume 64, Number 12, Births: Final Data for 2014. Published December 23, 2015. (http:wwwcdc,gov/nchs)

3   Caravan to Midnight podcast episode #446 aired January 8, 2016. (www.caravan to midnight.com)

4   https//www.goodreads.com/work/quotes-43 quotes from the book: *Velvet Elvis-Repainting the Christian Faith*

5   History of Portal 31. (www.portal/31.org/history_of_portal_31.htm

6   *The Steve Harvey Show,* Season 2, Episode170, air date: June 6, 2014

7   https//en.wikipedia.org/wiki/Civil_Rights_Actof1957

8   https:/ucr.fbi.gov/2012crime-in-the-us/2012/offenses-known-to-law-enforcement/expanded-homicide (Data Table 1)

9   The Ethical Demands for Integration, speech delivered in Nashville, Tennessee on December 27, 1962. From the book, "A Testament of Hope-The Essential Writings and Speeches of Martin Luther King, Jr, edited by James M Washington,

10 George Bernard Shaw, *Back to Methuselah,* act I, Selected Plays with Prefaces, Vol. 2, p.7 (1949)

11 http://www.jfklibrary.org/Research-Aids/Ready-Reference/RFK-Speeches/Day of Affirmation, June 6,1966

12 Thomas Sowell Syndicated Columnist Article Published February 4, 2015 Entitled: Obama vs America. (http//www.tsowell.com)

13 My Journey with Maya, by Travis Smiley, Chapter 5, p56, Copyright 2015, Hachette Book Group, Inc.

14 https://standingforgod.com/2012/12/09acknowledg-ing-gods-sovereignty

15 www.quotegarden.com/inner child-child,html,March18,1988

CPSIA information can be obtained
at www.ICGtesting.com
Printed in the USA
LVOW12s0021310816

502525LV00002B/4/P